DECODING ARTICLE 6 OF THE PARIS AGREEMENT

APRIL 2018

ASIAN DEVELOPMENT BANK

ADB

Notes:
In this publication, "$" refers to United States dollars.
Corrigenda to ADB publications may be found at http://www.adb.org/publications/corrigenda.

Contents

List of Figures and Box

FIGURES

BOX

The Asia and Pacific region has the largest number of climate-vulnerable people but also the highest overall potential for reducing greenhouse gas (GHG) emissions. The region could help bring about global transformation in line with the Paris Agreement, Sustainable Development Goals (SDGs), and the Sendai Framework for Disaster Risk Reduction 2015-2030 (Sendai Framework) to avoid adverse impacts of climate change.

Most of the developing member countries (DMCs) of the Asian Development Bank (ADB) have ratified the Paris Agreement to hold the increase in the global average temperature to less than 2°C above preindustrial levels, while aspiring to limit warming to 1.5°C. It is encouraging to note that DMCs are engaging in climate mitigation and adaptation interventions in line with their national climate plans and strategies, and have outlined their post-2020 nationally determined contributions (NDCs) under the Paris Agreement. Some of the recent developments, especially the significant growth in investments into renewable energy, highlight the fact that positive change is already happening, but not yet at the required pace. However, most mitigation targets set in the DMCs' NDCs generally depend, at least in part, on external financial and technical support for their achievement.

In 2015, ADB committed itself to increasing climate financing from its own resources to $6 billion yearly by 2020—$4 billion for mitigation in sectors such as renewable energy, energy efficiency, sustainable transport, and urban development, and $2 billion for adaptation in areas such as urban resilience and agriculture and land use. The $6 billion target corresponds to around 30% of ADB's projected corporate pipeline by 2020. In 2017, ADB has reached a record high of $4.5 billion in climate investments, a 21% increase from the $3.7 billion reached in 2016. From 2011 to 2017, ADB has approved more than $25 billion for climate financing—$21.7 billion from ADB's own resources while leveraging over $3.4 billion from external resources.

With a view to deliver stronger, better, and faster support to its DMCs, ADB has established its *Climate Change Operational Framework, 2017–2030 (CCOF 2030)*, which positions ADB to facilitate, collaboratively and proactively, a regional shift toward a low GHG emissions and climate-resilient development path. It further provides a framework for supporting DMCs in translating their NDC aspirations into climate change action investment plans and implementing those plans.

ADB remains steadfast in its engagement with carbon markets as it stands as one of the pillars of its climate change program. In line with CCOF 2030, ADB shall provide essential support to its DMCs through assisting in the design and development of new market mechanisms, the establishment and enhancement of domestic market mechanisms in their respective jurisdictions, and the implementation of an enhanced transparency framework including domestic implementation of monitoring, reporting, and verification, as well as accounting, as envisaged in the Paris Agreement.

The new framework for cooperative approaches and mechanisms under Article 6 of the Paris Agreement charts a path for the resurgence of carbon markets. However, the modalities, rules, and guidance are yet to be fully elaborated by the Parties to the Paris Agreement. This knowledge product closely examines these existing options and their corresponding implications for implementation.

As Asia and the Pacific faces mounting pressure to influence and take more concrete measures to reduce the impacts of climate change, it is my sincere hope that this publication will equip stakeholders and negotiators from developing countries, with a deeper understanding of the ongoing international discussions and technical options available for establishing the future carbon market guidance, rules, and modalities under Article 6 of the Paris Agreement.

Amy S.P. Leung
Director General
Sustainable Development and Climate Change Department
Asian Development Bank

Preface

In 2015, the Parties to the UN Framework Convention on Climate Change adopted the Paris Agreement, which is by far the most ambitious effort to strengthen the global response to address the challenges of climate change. Entered into force on 4 November 2016, the Paris Agreement has, for sure, inspired renewed interest in market mechanisms and enhanced expectations for the resurgence of carbon markets. Article 6 of the Paris Agreement is the new window of opportunity for market-based mechanisms and sets the framework for the post-2020 carbon markets at a regional and international level.

The new climate architecture gives countries the autonomy to develop their own ambitions or goals in the form of nationally determined contributions (NDCs) and approach(s) to achieve such ambitions include a wide range of policy instruments. Countries' achievements of their respective NDCs can be supplemented through the use of international cooperative approaches thus creating a framework to develop carbon markets.

The Paris Agreement was a momentous diplomatic achievement but needs a substantial amount of political and technical deliberations in the right earnest. The guidance, rules, modalities, and procedures for Article 6 and the rest of Paris Agreement are currently being negotiated among Parties, with the view of adopting the Paris rulebook at the 24th session of the Conference of the Parties (COP 24) in Katowice in Poland by the end of 2018.

Article 6 of the Paris Agreement comprises three approaches for cooperation between Parties - "cooperative approaches" under Article 6.2; a new mechanism to promote mitigation and sustainable development (Article 6.4 – 6.7); and a framework for non-market approaches (Article 6.8 and 6.9). There is, however, very little clarity on how these approaches will function and very basic issues such as scope, governance and infrastructure for operationalising provisions under Article 6 are still to be agreed. The scoping issues such as the eligible GHG mitigation activities in terms of their taking place inside and/or outside the host Party's NDC and eligible GHG gases are open for discussion. Under Article 6.2, Parties are yet to agree on what should be decided at the national level and at the international level, respectively.

Similarly, the relation between Article 6.2 and Article 6.4 needs to be clarified as Article 6.2 generally makes reference to Parties and the mechanism referred under Article 6.4 is under the authority of the Conference of the Parties Conference of the Parties serving as the meeting of the Parties to the Paris Agreement (CMA). Moreover, Parties need to discuss ways and means to ensure that double counting is avoided on the basis of corresponding adjustments which would require robust methods and procedures and the requisite infrastructure.

The negotiations so far have resulted in informal documents for each of the three Article 6 parts that contains identified options, however, a significant amount of work remains to resolve and agree upon options as well as their corresponding intricacies. Given that most of the technical issues in Articles 6.2, 6.4, and 6.8 are entwined with provisions under other articles of the Paris Agreement, its bearing on the progress should not surprise.

This publication comes at an important time as negotiators advance toward the finalization of the Paris rulebook at COP 24 to the UNFCCC. The forthcoming negotiations will be multilayered, involving the relation between Article 6 and other provisions of the Paris Agreement, such as the enhanced transparency framework that entails requirements for national inventories and reporting, and Article 4 which requires Parties to account for domestic and international efforts.

It is our hope that this publication will be useful to build an in-depth understanding of Article 6 and engage fruitful discussions among stakeholders to further shape climate actions and enable DMCs to contribute to the development and eventually take advantage of the new carbon markets under the Paris Agreement to accomplish targets under their respective NDCs.

Preety Bhandari
Director, Climate Change and Disaster Risk Management (CCDRM) Division and Chief of CCDRM Thematic Group, Sustainable Development and Climate Change Department Asian Development Bank

Virender Kumar Duggal
Principal Climate Change Specialist Fund Manager-Future Carbon Fund Sustainable Development and Climate Change Department Asian Development Bank

Acknowledgments

This knowledge product has been developed by the Technical Support Facility under Asian Development Bank's Carbon Market Program within its Sustainable Development and Climate Change Department.

Virender Kumar Duggal, principal climate change specialist, Climate Change and Disaster Risk Division, conceptualized and guided its development.

The knowledge product has been developed with technical inputs from a team of experts engaged under ADB's Technical Support Facility which included Mr. Andrei Marcu who contributed to the sections pertaining to market mechanisms (Article 6.2 and 6.4) and Mr. Johan Nylander who contributed to the section on non-market approaches (article 6.8), all of which are greatly appreciated.

The preparation of this knowledge product has also benefitted from expert advice from Hanna-Mari Ahonen from the Government of Finland, which is sincerely commended.

The timely publication of this knowledge product was made possible by diligent inputs from Jess Alfonso Macasaet, Joseph Manglicmot, Layla Yasmin Amar, Jan Carlo dela Cruz, and Joel Pinaroc, which are sincerely thanked.

Abbreviations

APA	-	Ad Hoc Working Group on the Paris Agreement
AAUs	-	assigned amount units
CDM	-	Clean Development Mechanism
CER	-	certified emission reduction
CMA	-	Conference of the Parties serving as the meeting of the Parties to the Paris Agreement
COP	-	Conference of the Parties
CO_2e	-	carbon dioxide equivalent
DNA	-	designated national authority
ETS	-	emissions trading system
FMCP	-	facilitative, multilateral consideration of progress
ITMO	-	internationally transferred mitigation outcome
MPG	-	modalities, procedures, and guidelines
NDC	-	nationally determined contribution
NMA	-	non-market approaches
SBSTA	-	Subsidiary Body for Scientific and Technological Advice
TER	-	technical expert review
UNFCCC	-	United Nations Framework Convention on Climate Change

This technical paper explores negotiations of Article 6 of the Paris Agreement. Article 6 can be divided into four parts: Article 6.1, Article 6.2-6.3, Article 6.4-6.7 and Article 6.8. Negotiations were mandated by Decision 1/CP.21. Currently, negotiations are being undertaken through the Subsidiary Body for Scientific and Technological Advice (SBSTA) Agenda Item 11. The current state of negotiations, decided at the 23rd session of the Conference of the Parties (COP) in November is that the SBSTA Chair has launched informal documents, which will be discussed at SBSTA 48 to be held in April–May 2018. (The SBSTA documents are attached in Annex 1.) Article 6 negotiations are to be finalized in line with the rulebook to implement the Paris Agreement, in December 2018 at the 24th session of the COP.

Overview of Article 6 of the Paris Agreement

Article 6 of the Paris Agreement is generally referred to as the "markets article." While Article 6 garnered a strong constituency of support, it also attracted strong opposition during and since the negotiations of the Paris Agreement.

Labeling Article 6 as a "market article" is somewhat simplistic, and does not do it justice, as it is actually much more than that. It provides a framework for general cooperation in the implementation of the Paris Agreement and the nationally determined contributions (NDCs). More precise provisions in Article 6 create a framework that will enable the creation of an international carbon market. This will lead to a convergence of domestic carbon pricing approaches, including carbon markets.

ARTICLE 6

"1. Parties recognize that some Parties choose to pursue voluntary cooperation in the implementation of their nationally determined contributions to allow for higher ambition in their mitigation and adaptation actions and to promote sustainable development and environmental integrity.

2. Parties shall, where engaging on a voluntary basis in cooperative approaches that involve the use of internationally transferred mitigation outcomes towards nationally determined contributions, promote sustainable development and ensure environmental integrity and transparency, including in governance, and shall apply robust accounting to ensure, inter alia, the avoidance of double counting, consistent with guidance adopted by the Conference of the Parties serving as the meeting of the Parties to this Agreement.

3. The use of internationally transferred mitigation outcomes to achieve nationally determined contributions under this Agreement shall be voluntary and authorized by participating Parties.

4. A mechanism to contribute to the mitigation of greenhouse gas emissions and support sustainable development is hereby established under the authority and guidance of the Conference of the Parties serving as the meeting of the Parties to this Agreement for use by Parties on a voluntary basis. It shall be supervised by a body designated by the Conference of the Parties serving as the meeting of the Parties to this Agreement, and shall aim:

    (i)   To promote the mitigation of greenhouse gas emissions while fostering sustainable development;

    (ii)   To incentivize and facilitate participation in the mitigation of greenhouse gas emissions by public and private entities authorized by a Party;

    (iii)   To contribute to the reduction of emission levels in the host Party, which will benefit from mitigation activities resulting in emission reductions that can also be used by another Party to fulfil its nationally determined contribution; and

    (iv)   To deliver an overall mitigation in global emissions.

5. Emission reductions resulting from the mechanism referred to in paragraph 4 of this Article shall not be used to demonstrate achievement of the host Party's nationally determined contribution if used by another Party to demonstrate achievement of its nationally determined contribution.

6. The Conference of the Parties serving as the meeting of the Parties to this Agreement shall ensure that a share of the proceeds from activities under the mechanism referred to in paragraph 4 of this Article is used to cover administrative expenses as well as to assist developing country Parties that are particularly vulnerable to the adverse effects of climate change to meet the costs of adaptation.

7. The Conference of the Parties serving as the meeting of the Parties to this Agreement shall adopt rules, modalities and procedures for the mechanism referred to in paragraph 4 of this Article at its first session.

continued on next page

Box: continued

8. Parties recognize the importance of integrated, holistic and balanced non-market approaches being available to Parties to assist in the implementation of their nationally determined contributions, in the context of sustainable development and poverty eradication, in a coordinated and effective manner, including through, inter alia, mitigation, adaptation, finance, technology transfer and capacity-building, as appropriate. These approaches shall aim to:

(i)   Promote mitigation and adaptation ambition;

(ii) Enhance public and private sector participation in the implementation of nationally determined contributions; and

(iii) Enable opportunities for coordination across instruments and relevant institutional arrangements.

9. A framework for non-market approaches to sustainable development is hereby defined to promote the non-market approaches referred to in paragraph 8 of this Article."

Scope of Article 6 of the Paris Agreement

Article 6 covers a number of concepts:

(i)   **Paragraph 6.1.** This paragraph covers the general concept that Parties may choose, on a voluntary basis, to cooperate in the implementation of their NDCs. Article 6 is meant to cover all existing cases of cooperation, and others that may emerge in the future. It is important to mention that cooperation is noted, acknowledged, and recognized, rather than approved by a body under the Paris Agreement. This reinforces the decentralized and bottom-up nature and ethos of the Paris Agreement governance.

(ii) **Transfers of mitigation outcomes (paragraphs 6.2–6.3).** These paragraphs cover the concept that when Parties are involved in the specific case of Cooperative Approaches that involve mitigation outcomes being transferred internationally, they need to observe Conference of the Parties serving as the meeting of the Parties to the Paris Agreement (CMA) guidance on accounting. The paragraphs are not about markets, but about a framework on how to account for transfers between Parties. What is particularly important is that these are internationally transferred mitigation outcome (ITMO), which can be produced from any mitigation approaches (mechanism, procedure, or protocol), without any reference to the fact that the mechanism, procedure, or protocol needs to operate under the authority of the Conference of the Parties (COP). Essentially whatever Parties involved will agree. There is no limitation being introduced in these paragraphs in the Paris Agreement as to what constitutes an ITMO and this broad scope is supported by the "institutional memory" of the Paris Agreement negotiations. Should limitations be introduced, they will essentially be an additional "boundary" or limitation which Parties to the Paris Agreement agree in the operationalization of Article 6, but currently have no "hook" in the current text.

(iii) **Mechanism to contribute to mitigation and support sustainable development (paragraphs 6.4–6.7).** These paragraphs refer to the establishment of a mechanism to produce mitigation outcomes and support sustainable development, and which operates under the authority of the COP. It produces mitigation outcomes that can then be used to fulfill the NDC of another Party. One of the key issues currently under debate is whether the scope of these paragraphs is limited to a a mechanism like Clean Development Mechanism (CDM), or it is much broader in scope. This interpretation seems to receive support from the historical evolution of the text, from the submissions made so far under Article 6 under Subsidiary Body for Scientific and Technological Advice (SBSTA) Article 6, as well as from positions expressed in formal and informal discussions.

(iv) **Framework for non-market approaches (paragraphs 6.8–6.9).** The establishment of a framework for non-market approaches that will aim to achieve the three issues is outlined in Article 6.8. It is still largely unclear what will be covered under this part of Article 6, but some focus is starting to emerge. One area seems to be coordination of different non-market cooperation approaches. Alternative ideas that were put forward expressed views that Articles 6.8 and 6.9 should be complementary to other provisions in the Paris Agreement, including in Articles 6.2 to 6.7, to ensure the sustainability of mitigation approaches, as well as address issues of global competitiveness in a cooperative manner, hence a connection to Article 4.15 of the Paris Agreement.

It is important to recognize that when Parties were negotiating the Paris Agreement, they wanted to provide alternatives that they could use in cooperating internationally in implementing the Paris Agreement and their respective NDC.

The options for participating in markets in one more centralized, and another, less centralized governance mode, were provided in a very deliberate way, to allow Parties to have choices. While operationalizing the Paris Agreement, Parties will negotiate the details of all these paragraphs and will agree on the level of governance centralization for Articles 6.2 and 6.4.

Carbon Markets in the Context of Article 6 of the Paris Agreement

In discussing how markets may emerge from the provisions of Article 6, it is necessary to focus on what Articles 6.2 to 6.7 may trigger in terms of markets.

It is possible to see Articles 6.2 and 6.4 in silos, i.e., as different worlds that do not interact, or may interact in a limited way. This is based on the history and experience of the Kyoto Protocol mechanisms, CDM, Joint Implementation, and Article 17. In that case, Parties essentially used certified emission reductions (CERs) and emission reduction units (ERUs) for sovereign compliance with the Kyoto Protocol, or to meet obligations for domestic compliance, such as the European Union Emissions Trading System (ETS). The impact of the role of indirect linking that was attributed to CERs and ERUs during what can be called Carbon Markets 1.0, while not untrue, was much more limited in practice in terms of real market dynamics.

Given the divergence of views that will need to be bridged, both in terms of the legitimacy of issues to be included as well as the choices between the different options put forward by Parties, it may be useful to identify some basic principles to help in the review of these options.

(i) **Bottom-up.** The ethos of the Paris Agreement is bottom-up, and that should permeate thinking in making decisions. This is true in the determination of NDCs, and true in the governance that will be chosen.

(ii) **Governance.** While the governance is certainly much more decentralized than in the Kyoto Protocol, there will still be elements of centralization. However, the balance between centralization and decentralization is remarkably different from the Kyoto Protocol.

(iii) **Transparency.** Transparency plays a critical role in the governance of the Paris Agreement, and it is meant to create trust among Parties, as they aim to raise the level of ambition.

(iv) **Article 6 is unitary.** Article 6 elements cannot be considered in isolation, they need to be considered together. One view is that Articles 6.2 and 6.4 were put forward as options, with different governance, for Parties to cooperate internationally. Mitigation activities are not pegged into Articles 6.2 or 6.4, it is more likely that Parties should have a choice between Article 6.2 and Article 6.4.

(v) **The Paris Agreement is unitary.** Article 6 must not be seen in isolation, but in the context of the Paris Agreement in its entirety. Sustainable development, transparency, environmental integrity, and accounting are not only present in Article 6, but throughout the Paris Agreement. Article 6 will have to build on and be connected with Articles 4, 13, and 15. At the same time, Article 6 will also inform the more general Paris Agreement framework, including Article 13.7—information "to track progress," which will necessarily include information with respect to the use of ITMOs pursuant to Article 6.2. Article 6.2, including arrangements for "corresponding adjustment" may also inform the format and timing of that information under Article 13.7.

Comparing Markets under Paris Agreement and Kyoto Protocol

The Kyoto Protocol and the Paris Agreement differ in their approaches to carbon market mechanisms.

The Kyoto Protocol is based on the principle that developed countries should take the lead in combatting climate change which was operationalized through setting GHG emission reduction targets for these countries. The developing countries did not take on quantitative targets.

In the Paris Agreement, the situation is different since all countries have to submit Nationally Determined Contributions (NDCs) as part of the joint effort to reach the overall objective of the Agreement. However, there is a variety in terms of types of NDCs implying that compared to the Kyoto Protocol where developed countries had the same type of target, the Paris Agreement contains different types of targets.

The compliance systems are also different. Under Kyoto, there are legally binding targets for developed countries, with a strict compliance system, overseen by a compliance committee. The whole system is centralized, top-down.

In the Paris Agreement, the key element for compliance is transparency, where Parties show what they plan to do and how they have done it. Central to this system is a global stocktake where Parties assess their common effort toward the common objective.

In the Kyoto Protocol, flexible mechanisms were introduced to create flexibility for the countries to meet their targets. International Emissions Trading (Article 17) provides for trade between countries with caps, Joint Implementation (Article 6) defines a project-based mechanism for verifying emission reductions in countries with caps, and Clean Development Mechanism (CDM) was established for creating verified emission reductions in countries without targets.

Countries wishing to participate in emissions trading would have to meet eligibility criteria, including taking on an economy wide GHG reduction target. Developing countries can participate in the carbon market as hosts of CDM projects. The framework for carbon trading thus contained one system for developed countries, and another system for developing countries.

Under the Paris Agreement, countries can potentially participate in the carbon market and be potential seller or buyers of mitigation outcomes. Depending on a country's preferences, it may choose from a more centralized approach using a centrally overseen mechanism (Article 6.4) or a less centralized approach (Article 6.2) under which countries define approaches or mechanisms, although how less centralized is yet to be agreed. The Kyoto Protocol is less flexible in these terms. However, under JI developed countries can choose a centralized route (Track II) that includes a validation and verification process overseen by a UN body, the JI Supervisory Committee, or they can choose to apply a national verification process (Track 1). Track 2 was established as an alternative for JI host countries that do not fulfill all eligibility requirements from the outset.

It can be argued that Article 6.2 has similarities with Article 17 of the Paris Agreement in that it may provide for international emissions trading, but it also could include a JI-like approach (Track 1). Article 6.4 is often mentioned as a successor to CDM but would also remind of JI Track 2. The fact is that there is no one-to-one match between the approaches under the Kyoto Protocol with the approaches under the Paris Agreement, as illustrated in the Table.

	Kyoto Protocol	Paris Agreement
Scope	**Article 6/ Article 17**	**Article 6.2**
	• JI/International Emissions Trading	• Cooperative Approaches
	Article 12	**Article 6.4**
	• CDM	• Mechanism for Mitigation and Sustainable Development
		Article 6.8
		• Framework for Non-Market Approaches
International oversight	**Mainly centralized**	**Mainly centralized**
	• Article 12 (CDM)	• Article 6.4
	Mainly decentralized	**Mainly decentralized**
	• Article 17 • Article 6 (JI Track I)	• Article 6.2
	Some centralization • Article 6 (JI Track II)	
Scale of activity	**Projects / Programs**	**Projects / Programs/Policy instruments / Sectors**
	• Article 12 (CDM) • Article 6 (JI Track I and Track II)	• Article 6.2 • Article 6.4 • Article 6.8
	Sectors	
	• Article 17 (International Emissions Trading)	
Governance	**Article 17**	**Article 6.2**
	• Supervision by the UNFCCC Compliance committee	• No body
	Article 12 (CDM)	**Article 6.4**
	• CDM Executive Board	• A body to be designated
	Article 6 (JI Track I)	
	• Supervision by the UNFCCC Compliance committee	
	Article 6 (JI Track II)	
	• JI Supervisory Committee	
Transparency and reporting	**Article 17**	**Article 6.2**
	• Kyoto Protocol compliance system	• Reporting through transparency framework • Corresponding Adjustments
	Article 12 (CDM)	**Article 6.4**
	• Centrally under UNFCCC	• Centrally under UNFCCC • Reporting through transparency framework
	Article 6 (JI Track I)	
	• Kyoto Protocol compliance system	
	Article 6 (JI Track II)	
	• Centrally under UNFCCC	

Disclaimer: The box represents a simplification for illustration purposes and does not present all options and proposals by Parties. The box should also not be seen as prejudging any outcome of ongoing negotiations. The columns should be read independently.

Environmental Integrity in Article 6.2

ARTICLE 6.2

"Parties shall, where engaging on a voluntary basis in cooperative approaches that involve the use of internationally transferred mitigation outcomes towards nationally determined contributions, promote sustainable development and ensure environmental integrity and transparency, including in governance, and shall apply robust accounting to ensure, inter alia, the avoidance of double counting, consistent with guidance adopted by the Conference of the Parties serving as the meeting of the Parties to this Agreement."

1. Issues for Discussion

Article 6.2 includes a number of "shall" provisions and states that "Parties shall, where engaging on a voluntary basis in Cooperative Approaches [...] ensure environmental integrity [...] including in governance."

There is therefore a clear provision on environmental integrity in Article 6.2, which is not contested by Parties. However, there is still considerable ambiguity concerning how this provision is to be operationalized, and what its governance will be. There is also no explicit work program associated with it in decision 1/CP.21.

Given these facts, the issues still under discussion on environmental integrity include:

- How can environmental integrity be defined?
- How should environmental integrity be operationalized?
- What is the governance that needs to be put in place?

This paper aims to address these three issues in light of the recent Party submissions, and both formal and informal discussions among negotiators on the topic, as well as the co-facilitator's informal note from the Subsidiary Body for Scientific and Technological Advice 47.

2. Environmental Integrity

It is important to note that the way these issues are addressed may have an impact on the scope of Article 6.2, that is, how much diversity Article 6.2 will support.

Currently, there is no generally accepted definition of environmental integrity, and given the diversity of nationally determined contributions (NDCs) and the type of internationally transferred mitigation outcomes (ITMOs) that may emerge (depending on the scope of Article 6.2), it may be challenging to come up with a generally accepted definition.

While defining environmental integrity is difficult, one view is that it encompasses more than just ITMOs. Many Parties see it as an overarching goal for the entire Paris Agreement. In this view, environmental integrity is a systemic issue, which requires a systemic approach to ensure it, including various elements such as robust accounting, monitoring, and clear transparency and reporting rules, not restricted to the Article 6 framework only.

In their submissions, as well as during (in)formal negotiations, a number of requirements have been raised by Parties for ensuring the environmental integrity of the cooperative mechanism of Article 6.2:

- Creation or transfer of ITMOs shall not result in a net increase in global emissions.
- ITMOs shall be real, permanent, additional, measurable, and quantifiable.
- ITMOs will result from activities where the reference to calculate emission reductions shall be set well below business-as-usual levels of the specific sector.
- ITMOs will not result in environmental harm and avoid conflict with other environmental-related aspects.
- No hot air is created by creating or transferring ITMOs.
- No leakage occurs when creating or transferring ITMOs.

Based on these suggested requirements, environmental integrity, could loosely be defined as: ensuring that a transfer done under Article 6.2 does not impact the atmosphere in a negative way while aiding to reach the overall goals of the Paris Agreement.

However, some Parties propose a definition that goes further than not impacting the atmosphere in a negative way. Keeping in mind the goal of achieving higher ambition, as stipulated in Article 6.1, some Parties are of the opinion that the Cooperative Approaches under Article 6.2 should result in a greater level of mitigation than would have occurred otherwise, and thus cause an overall reduction of global emissions, therefore making a positive impact on the atmosphere.

Three main views regarding the definition of environmental integrity may be seen as emerging from submissions, as well as formal and informal discussions. The three views could be translated as "what does environmental integrity mean in the context of Article 6.2?" These views are not unrelated to the discussions regarding the scope of Article 6.2.

- **View 1.** Environmental integrity only covers the transfer, that is, how you ensure that the transfer of an ITMO is represented in an accurate way and meets the definition presented here. In this case, what (i.e., the quality or characteristics of what you transfer) you transfer is a bilateral or plurilateral issue between the Parties involved in the transfer.
- **View 2.** Environmental integrity covers how you transfer an ITMO, as well as what you transfer. In this view, an ITMO should meet certain environmental characteristics.

- **View 3.** Environmental integrity covers, like view 2, both how and what you transfer, but can be seen as a more structured or defined approach. For illustration purposes, as other options may emerge, this view could argue that only units that are clearly defined and issued by the United Nations (UN) can be transferred.

Three types of arguments have emerged from informal discussions in support of View 1. Some Parties are of the opinion that ensuring environmental integrity is a part of the environmental pillar of sustainable development. Since defining and promoting sustainable development is widely viewed as a national prerogative of the Parties, it is argued that defining and ensuring the environmental integrity of an ITMO falls within this national prerogative.

Others argue that the guidance referred to in Article 6.2 only applies to robust accounting, and that the mandate given to the SBSTA in decision 1/CP.21 is limited only to developing and recommending guidance on accounting, including corresponding adjustments.

A third reasoning builds upon the difficulties in defining environmental integrity as previously discussed: it is argued that in light of the big variety in the types of NDCs, it would be fruitless to attempt to define environmental integrity. Another part of the argument is that environmental integrity should be ensured as best as possible with guidance on robust accounting and corresponding adjustments.

With respect to View 2, three different approaches can be identified to achieve the goal of ensuring the environmental integrity of ITMOs. Some argue that the guidance referred to in Article 6.2 should be limited to overall, broad principles for ensuring environmental integrity. Based on these principles, Parties themselves can individually make guidelines that ITMOs should meet.

Others argue that principles do not go far enough, and that such guidelines should be formulated multilaterally by the Parties. A third group goes even further, and would like to see the emergence of more rigid rules or criteria that ITMOs should meet and can be tested for (possibly by a body under the CMA).

View 3 has been discussed to a lesser extent but comes directly from Party submissions. This view argues that environmental integrity is primarily ensured by the certainty that comes from the atmospheric value of what is being transferred. It must be made sure that the face value of a unit (e.g., 1 ton of carbon dioxide equivalent) reflects its real atmospheric value. As such, ITMOs need to be expressed in units well understood and whose atmospheric value the UN is certain of.

An additional element raised by Parties does not fit exclusively in any of the three views. As previously mentioned, some Parties are proponents of a definition of environmental integrity in the context of Article 6.2 that, ensures the goal of raising ambition, in the way that the Cooperative Approaches should result in a net-positive effect on the atmosphere. Proponents of this view make the connection with the concept of "overall mitigation" which, should also be a goal of Article 6.2. However, the concept of overall mitigation is only mentioned in Article 6.4, and is not in the text of Article 6.2, nor in its work program.

3.   Operationalization

In terms of the operationalization of the views outlined above, all three recognize, also with regard to ensuring environmental integrity, the need for guidance on robust accounting and corresponding adjustments.

For some Parties, this guidance on accounting should include limitations for the transfer, or use, of ITMOs to mitigate the risk posed by overselling or overusing. Overselling could endanger NDC achievement, while overusing would be contrary to the principle of supplementarity. These Parties argue that mitigating these risks are also key to ensuring environmental integrity. They advocate the adoption of restrictions regarding the amount of ITMOs that can be transferred by a Party or limitations on the amount of ITMOs that can be used toward a Party's NDC (either in absolute quantities or relative percentages).

View 1 is operationalized in the Paris Agreement through accounting provisions, including corresponding adjustments, and transparency provisions under Article 13 of the Paris Agreement, the enhanced transparency framework. Parties advocating this view argue that these are sufficient, and no additional transparency provisions in the context of Article 6.2 are necessary. They stress that Parties will have their own criteria for ensuring the environmental integrity of an ITMO, and that the bilateral and plurilateral aspect of Article 6.2 will ensure a check for environmental integrity. Hence, when participating in Cooperative Approaches, Parties will have environmental integrity standards and will be transparent to each other about these standards, as well as to the international community through the enhanced transparency framework. Proponents of this view argue that this will put significant pressure on Parties to ensure environmental integrity.

View 2 sees environmental integrity in the Paris Agreement through (i) accounting provisions; (ii) provisions for environmental integrity, potentially in the form of "guidance" or criteria; and (iii) transparency provisions, including additional disclosure provisions on how the ITMOs meet the CMA "guidance" on environmental integrity. Another provision that may also be added is in the form of a technical (peer) review process.

The overall goal would be to get a clear picture of the characteristics of the ITMO whether or not it meets the CMA "guidance" and allow third Parties to form a judgement if they are being met. Who checks on meeting these standards is an issue that will have to be addressed under governance.

Within this view, there is also a debate as to where these additional transparency and reporting rules should be situated. While some argue that these should be drafted and included in the context of the guidance for Article 6.2, as decided in 1/CP.21, others are of the opinion that such rules should be added to the enhanced transparency framework in Article 13.

Parties preferring this second option argue that Article 6 negotiators lack the necessary expertise to draft transparency rules themselves, and that doing so could endanger the coherence between the different articles in the Paris Agreement. In this view, a "placeholder" would be left in the enhanced transparency framework for the additional transparency or reporting rules of the Article 6.2 mechanism, which would be drafted by the Article 13 experts, based on the inputs from the Article 6 negotiators.

View 3 argues that when Parties want to engage in the Cooperative Approach under Article 6.2, standards for ITMOs should be CMA defined, and adherence to these standards checked by the CMA. One submission does see ITMOs as units with well-defined environmental characteristics, developed under the CMA, and only emerging from NDCs quantified into a budget. In this case, a number of units (similar to the assigned amount units [AAUs] under the Kyoto Protocol) would be issued.

4.   Governance

In terms of the overall governance of Article 6, four possible regimes can be envisioned, which would both influence Article 6.2, as well as be influenced by the governance of Article 6.2:

(i)   A broadly decentralized climate change regime without any global standards for environmental integrity. Countries are free to use any international mitigation outcomes they choose for compliance; this is in line with View 1. In this case, there are also no special transparency provisions on the environmental integrity of ITMOs defined by the CMA.

(ii)   A decentralized climate change regime with some minimum environmental standards provided by the CMA, as guidance only. The CMA would provide these principles or guidelines, but would not check if they are met; this can be seen as an option under View 2. In this case, there are also no special transparency provisions for the environmental integrity of ITMOs issued by the CMA.

(iii)   A climate change regime where the environmental standards, set out by the CMA, must be observed, but no "testing and approval" is envisaged and required for the ITMOs to be used toward NDCs. This can also be seen as an option under View 2 of addressing environmental integrity under Article 6.2. In this case, the CMA includes, either in Article 6.2 or in the enhanced transparency framework, special provisions for disclosure of environmental integrity of ITMOs. The CMA may also define and add a technical peer review process.

(iv)   A centralized governance regime: global environmental standards are defined by the CMA, and must be observed. The CMA approves units (or mitigation outcomes) or the systems that produce units (or mitigation outcomes) used for the United Nations Framework Convention on Climate Change (UNFCCC) compliance; this can be seen in accordance with View 3 (or a strong version of View 2).

The four regimes outlined above need to be seen as an attempt to group together options, and the reader may see "in between options." This is not meant to be negotiating text.

Parties leaning toward the first option stress that a decentralized regime does not imply that there are no checks. Since the mechanism under Article 6.2 is characterized by cooperation, Parties will still be able to check each other, bilaterally or plurilaterally, when applicable. Transparency and reporting under Article 13 is sufficient in their view, and the key tool to "name and shame" Parties who fail to ensure environmental integrity.

Some supporters of View 2 put most emphasis on the central role of strong, additional rules for transparency and reporting on the additional principles, guidelines, or criteria formulated by the CMA. They put less emphasis on the potential role of a body, such as the CMA, to check for compliance.

However, other Parties argue that the guidance or criteria for Article 6.2 should be subject to a technical review by experts, possibly as part of the enhanced transparency framework. Consent for the compliance with these guidelines or criteria will have to be obtained from this technical review committee before the specific ITMO can be transferred or used toward a Party's NDC.

Interestingly, some Parties envision a progressive role for the CMA. Under this view, the UNFCCC, through the CMA, or a designated body, should start with the role of providing facilities for review and discussion. Over time, the CMA, or a designated body, may be given additional competencies and roles by the Parties, or decide on additional guidance where it deems it to be necessary.

Scope of Article 6.2

ARTICLE 6.2

"Parties shall, where engaging on a voluntary basis in cooperative approaches that involve the use of internationally transferred mitigation outcomes towards nationally determined contributions, promote sustainable development and ensure environmental integrity and transparency, including in governance, and shall apply robust accounting to ensure, inter alia, the avoidance of double counting, consistent with guidance adopted by the Conference of the Parties serving as the meeting of the Parties to this Agreement."

1. Defining the Scope of Article 6.2

The scope of Article 6.2 is understood, for the purpose of this paper, to be the type of activities, mitigation actions, and transfers covered by the article. It also includes the degree to which Parties (and those authorized by Parties) will use Article 6.2. Defining the scope of Article 6.2 will require several questions to be answered, which are related to the limitations that can be introduced.

One issue is what can be transferred, that is, what is the nature of an internationally transferred mitigation outcome (ITMO)? By limiting the ITMOs, through quality or quantity, we limit the scope of Article 6.2.

A second limitation could emanate from who can transfer ITMOs. By limiting or creating conditionalities on who can transfer ITMOs, the scope of Article 6.2 will also automatically be limited.

This paper addresses these questions, and reviews some of the choices that will need to be made for the operationalization of Article 6.2.

2. Why Is Scope an Issue?

The question of the scope of Article 6.2 is particularly important because it may impact the ability of Parties to cooperate in any particular manner. Limitations imposed upon its scope will inevitably also impact the bottom-up ethos of the Paris Agreement. This will be a decision that will be driven by political considerations, as well as practical ones, given the need to address and operationalize other provisions in the Paris Agreement, including on accounting, corresponding adjustments, environmental integrity, etc.

At first glance, the scope of Article 6.2 seems broad, as there is no explicit qualifier restricting its use to mechanisms under the authority of the Conference of the Parties serving as the meeting of the Parties to the Paris Agreement (CMA).

Article 6.2 could therefore be taken to cover any type of cooperation, including transfers between national or regional emissions trading systems (ETS), within Joint Crediting Mechanism (JCM)-type cooperation mechanisms, Article 6.4 outcomes, and any other mitigation outcomes created under domestic or plurilateral jurisdiction.

If Article 6.2 thus seems to offer relative flexibility to Parties, some potential limitations do nevertheless exist. These limitations could be classified into two categories.

Explicit limitations. Article 6.2 of the Paris Agreement includes what could be deemed as explicit potential limitations. This includes provisions to ensure that when Parties use ITMOs toward their nationally determined contributions (NDCs), they "shall...promote sustainable development and ensure environmental integrity and transparency, including in governance," and "shall...apply robust accounting." Whether sustainable development, environmental integrity, and robust accounting turn out to be significant limiting elements to the scope of Article 6.2 or not will largely depend on how these "shall provisions" are operationalized and what their governance will be. These are issues that have yet to be settled in negotiations.

Another explicit limitation may come from Article 6.3, which accompanies Article 6.2 and states that the use of ITMOs toward NDCs shall be "voluntary and authorized by participating Parties." This is not dissimilar to the Clean Development Mechanism (CDM) and Joint Implementation provisions in the Kyoto Protocol, and the extent to which it will limit the scope of Article 6.2 will also depend on its governance and the way it is operationalized.

Implicit limitations. Other limitations could be seen as implicit or emerging from an interpretation of the text of Article 6.2. This includes three potential set of limitations.

The first potential set of limitations could cover the object of the transfer—what can be transferred. This set of limitations could include

- restrictions on whether the mitigation outcome originates from inside or outside the NDC in terms of sector, gases, or vintages);
- requirements on the quality of ITMO, in terms of environmental integrity and sustainable development;
- quantity restrictions, referring to the amount that can be transferred and used toward NDCs;
- metrics in which the ITMO is determined in; and
- possible restrictions emanating from the relationship, yet to be defined, between Articles 6.2 and 6.4.

The second limitation may refer to who can transfer, that is, any eligibility criteria. There were eligibility criteria related to Articles 6, 12, and 17 of the Kyoto Protocol, so it is not unnatural to raise this issue. In particular, it will be important to determine if Parties with any type of NDC will be able to engage in transfers under Article 6.2.

A final type of implicit limitation, which refers to the issuance, use, and characteristics of an ITMO, would gather a wide variety of provisions. The introduction of share of proceeds, depending on how it is done, could create a disincentive effect for the transfer of ITMOs.

An overall mitigation clause could have the same effect: if the use of ITMOs toward NDC must be less than the actual amount abated, this could well disincentivize Parties from issuing, transferring, and/or using ITMOs.

Similar considerations could accompany limitations of the shelf life of ITMOs, or the creation of a Kyoto Protocol-like Commitment Period Reserve.

Any provisions regarding the timing of accounting and corresponding adjustment that create uncertainty, during a certain period, as to who possesses the ITMO and who will use it, may for the same reason be considered an implicit limitation. Although very different in nature, all these put limits on Article 6.2. They are meant by their promoters to address different issues, many worthwhile, but they all, in reality, impose limitations on the use of Article 6 and the market it creates.

Whether or not these implicit limitations materialize will depend on what emerges from the negotiations: is Article 6.2 dealing only with the transfer of ITMOs, or is Article 6.2 also dealing with the creation and use of the ITMO (i.e., accounting toward NDC)?

3.   Considerations on the Scope of Article 6.2

3.1   Commoditization

One definition of a commodity is a basic good used in commerce that is interchangeable with other commodities of the same type. In this sense, the Kyoto Protocol created a number of tradable commodities (assigned amount units, certified emission reductions, emission reduction units), the key building blocks for a carbon market.

Article 6.2 of the Paris Agreement may open a similar window for a global carbon market. However, in the case of Article 6.2, no commodity is being explicitly created. Some see ITMOs as new units for transfer; in this paper ITMOs are considered as units of accounting.

One possible scenario may be that many types of ITMOs would emerge, each with different characteristics and metrics. These different units may converge over time. An alternative interpretation sees ITMOs as being a commodity from the beginning, standardized through agreement among Parties.

It is important to also examine the consequences of either scenario. Rules, which would impose or accelerate commodification of ITMOs, will speed up convergence toward a global carbon price, and the creation of a global carbon market. This is deemed by many to be needed, and desirable.

However, such rules will inevitably limit the scope of Article 6.2 and impact the bottom-up ethos of the Paris Agreement. There is a tension, maybe positive, between on the one hand the bottom-up ethos and the wide scope of Article 6.2 it implies, and on the other hand the goal of having a global commodity.

This tension informs the whole debate on Article 6, and its resolution will perhaps be the central challenge that will be faced by Article 6 negotiators in the coming years. The decision will be driven by multitude practical aspects related to the implementation of Article 6, including the wide range of ways in which NDCs are expressed.

3.2   Impact of Governance

Article 6.2 is generally associated with decentralized governance, at least when contrasted with the modalities and procedures that are foreseen for Article 6.4, and in the Kyoto Protocol mechanisms. This decentralization will tend to allow for a broad scope, as each Party is free to define what an ITMO is. Over time, it is inevitable that we may see convergence and the emergence of some "common standard."

The choice of more centralized governance from the beginning will likely result in an immediate limitation of the scope, and ITMOs will be commoditized faster.

Some Parties have instead suggested it may be wise to consider the elaboration of governance as an evolutionary process. If there is some level of initial centralization through the CMA guidance, Parties should not necessarily consider this a one-shot process of "get it right or fail." Instead, establishing the governance of the Article could be taken as a long-term evolutionary process, in which the governance itself includes provisions for a cycle of reviews. Some limited, centralized guidance would be developed, and then further provisions would be added if it were found that particular standards developed by some Parties are useful.

Other Parties have highlighted that the definition of centralization is itself not clear, as it could imply a central CMA-type governing body, or some common rules applying to everyone. Given the different understandings of the word, and the fact that Parties often adhere to more nuanced positions that do not fall in the strict dichotomy of centralized vs. decentralized, these strict categories have sometimes been deemed to be unhelpful. It has thus been suggested that the discussions may be more fruitful if Parties start by envisaging the actual operationalization elements, rather than enter a centralized vs. decentralized governance debate.

4.   Limitations on the Scope of Article 6.2

What distinguishes Article 6 from the rest of the Paris Agreement is its focus on international cooperation. Article 6.2 focuses on the particular case of cooperation through transfers between Parties.

Since this is a "transfer article," any discussion on "limitation to the scope of Article 6.2" may be interpreted as referring primarily to the transfer aspect, and not other aspects. However, three broad dimensions of such limitations can be identified, with significant overlap in the considerations affecting each of them:

- limitations on *what* can be transferred;
- limitations on *who* can transfer; and
- limitations on the *transfer itself.*

4.1   What Can Be Transferred?

4.1.1   Inside–Outside the Scope of a Nationally Determined Contribution

Whether or not a mitigation outcome originating from a sector currently outside the scope of a Party's NDC can be transferred under Article 6.2 is a contentious issue. Some Parties have expressed the view that if a Party desires to transfer a mitigation outcome from such a sector, it must first expand the scope of its NDC to encompass that sector.

Other Parties, however, have difficulties with this option. It is argued that Article 6.2 is supposed to foster ambition, not restrain it. It is therefore important not to discourage national efforts in sectors that are not currently within the NDC.

On the contrary, if a Party knows a mitigation outcome can be transferred internationally, even if it is outside the scope of its NDC, this may encourage action in these sectors and promote, in future NDC rounds, the broadening of its scope, eventually, toward an economy-wide NDC.

The concept of transfers of mitigation outcomes from sectors outside the scope of an NDC has also raised concerns about double counting and corresponding adjustments. With respect to double counting, a transfer from outside the scope of an NDC does not seem to pose double counting issues, as the mitigation outcome can only be counted in the NDC of the receiving country.

Double counting will only become an issue if, in the next round of NDCs, pursuing activities in that area has encouraged the host Party to enlarge the scope of its NDC to include that sector. The mitigation outcome that has been transferred cannot then be counted by the host Party because otherwise, double counting will indeed occur. With respect to corresponding adjustments, the question of what to adjust is an evident one, and not answered so far.

The inside–outside debate also extends beyond the sector question. It first also arises in terms of greenhouse gases. When identifying the source of ITMOs that may be internationally transferred, and used toward a Party's NDC, the mitigation outcome could be required to represent a reduction or avoidance of emissions of a gas that is itself covered by the host Party's NDC.

A more flexible stance would allow the transfer and use toward NDCs of a mitigation outcome derived from the emission reduction or avoidance of any greenhouse gas, whether inside or outside the host Party's NDC. Adopting the first view would result in restricting the scope of Article 6.2.

The inside–outside debate also arises in terms of vintages of ITMOs. For single year NDCs, it has been proposed that, for the issuing party, the international transfer of ITMOs be limited to mitigation in the NDC target year. For the using party, it has been proposed that the use of ITMOs be limited to those with the same vintage as the NDC target year. Such inside–outside considerations, this time in terms of vintages, could once again have scope-limiting implications.

Finally, one important aspect that merits to be mentioned is that some Parties consider "beyond the scope of NDC", which would include outside the scope of the NDC, in the case of Article 6.4, as additional.

4.1.2   Quality of the Internationally Transferred Mitigation Outcome

It is the view of some Parties that only ITMOs of a certain quality can be used toward NDCs. In particular, it is considered that ITMOs should meet certain standards of environmental integrity and sustainable development. The Article indeed explicitly states that Parties "shall," when cooperating through the transfer of ITMOs, promote sustainable development and ensure environmental integrity. These two elements are thus certainly candidates to being scope-limiting factors.

The issue is contentious, as other Parties insist the article do not elevate these two elements to the rank of potential constraints. They insist that the guidance to be developed by the CMA is for accounting only, and not for environmental integrity or sustainable development. The accounting is not "subject to guidance," but "consistent with guidance." The choice of the word "guidance," could also play an important role. In contrast to more binding terminology, such as "rules," guidance is seen as only being there to help implementation, not to impose constraints on the use of the article.

This view is disputed, as there is a strong feeling among many Parties that environmental integrity is an overarching priority, and that it must be ensured that transfers under Article 6.2 do not undermine the goals of the Paris Agreement. Some Parties thus argue that the guidance referred to in Article 6.2 and decision 1/CP.21 covers both environmental integrity as well as accounting.

Resolving this issue will be particularly difficult, given that Parties do not agree on what environmental integrity means in the context of Article 6.2.

One view is that environmental integrity only covers the transfer, that is, how to ensure that the transfer of an ITMO is represented in an accurate way. In this case, what you transfer (i.e., the quality or characteristics of what you transfer) is a bilateral or plurilateral issue between the Parties involved in the transfer.

Another view is that environmental integrity covers both how you transfer an ITMO, as well as what you transfer. In this view, an ITMO should meet certain environmental characteristics. One of these characteristics could be additionality: the informal note from the Subsidiary Body for Scientific and Technological Advice (SBSTA) co-facilitators mentions "evidence that ITMO is real, permanent, additional, and verified.".[1] If it were to become a requirement, it would have severe scope-limiting implications because it only applies to baseline-and-credit approaches traditionally in the UNFCCC discourse.

Yet another view is that environmental integrity covers both how and what you transfer, but in a more structured and defined approach. For illustration purposes, as other options may emerge, this view could argue that only UN-issued, clearly defined units (e.g., in tons of carbon dioxide equivalent [CO_2e]) can be transferred. In this case ITMOs become tradable units from accounting units.

The issue of sustainable development is somewhat less contentious, as it is clear from many submissions that sustainable development is viewed as a national prerogative. Many submissions take the view that it is not the role of the international community to define national sustainable development priorities. This is by no means universally accepted by those who point to the Sustainable Development Goals.

The view has also been expressed that even if sustainable development is a national prerogative, it does not impede the buyer of an ITMO to look at the conditions under which these ITMOs were produced. The Party in question could select its source of ITMOs on the standards under which they were produced. Sustainable development, if it is unlikely to emerge as a strong limitation, could well become the object of reporting practices.

Finally, concerns over the quality of ITMO have led some Parties to propose restrictions in sectors with a high degree of uncertainty in emission reductions, and that only ITMOs generated post 2020 may be used.

4.1.3   Type of the Internationally Transferred Mitigation Option
Submissions present two opposing views with respect to the type of ITMOs that can be transferred. As always, there are also in-between views.

The first view claims that as Article 6.2 refers to voluntary international cooperation; ITMOs can be whatever the Parties involved in the transfer desire. Article 6.2 would thus have few fences. It could potentially cover a wide variety of transfers and mechanisms, including transfers between ETS, energy certificates trading schemes, Reducing Emissions from Deforestation and Degradation, etc.

One could find support for that view in the existence, in some early drafts of the Paris Agreement (e.g., 30 November 2015 draft), of references to additionality. The presence of such provisions would have implied that only ITMOs resulting from baseline-and-credit approaches (where the additionality concept is relevant) could be transferred under Article 6.2. Removal of all mention of additionality suggests a broad interpretation of Article 6.2 could be legitimate.

[1]   Paragraph 6.g, Informal Note by the co-chairs on Article 6, paragraph 2. 12 November 2017

The second interpretation, however, holds that for Parties to transfer mitigation outcomes and count them toward their NDCs, ITMOs must meet some criteria. Indeed, the remaining Parties must have the assurance that the unit transferred is equivalent to 1 ton of CO_2e in atmospheric terms. The implementation of such a view can take two forms. The CMA, or another UN body, could verify every type of unit issued nationally, which implies a strong intrusion in domestic climate policies.

A second option is to only accept, under Article 6.2, the transfer of internationally recognized units. This is the view defended by some Parties, and names for such units have been proposed (e.g., Quantified Contribution Unit).

This second interpretation is typically accompanied by a proposal for ITMOs to be denominated in tons of carbon dioxide equivalent, although Parties that do not subscribe to the second interpretation have also proposed this.

Various reasons could be invoked for the imposition of a carbon metric: Parties are used to this approach from the Kyoto Protocol; it makes accounting significantly easier; and it directly creates commodities. However, imposing a carbon metric would severely limit the scope of Article 6.2, as Parties could not exchange other types of ITMOs, e.g., renewable certificates, to use toward their NDC.

It would certainly be possible to convert ITMOs from NDCs not expressed in carbon dioxide equivalent (CO_2e) into CO_2e. In that case, the conversion factor would have to be determined, possibly at both ends of the transfer if both NDCs are not expressed in CO_2e. Who would determine such a conversion factor would have to be agreed upon: national authorities or a body under the CMA.

A variation on the CO_2e-denominated ITMO position, which has been proposed by some Parties, would consider ITMOs to be not the commodity transferred itself, but the net flows between Parties, measured in tons of CO_2e. This is a very different conception of an ITMO, which would have significant implications in terms of accounting, yet it does not seem to have additional scope-limiting implications.

It must be emphasized that many Parties and others stakeholders do not fall in either of the two "extreme" positions. They have argued that there is a middle ground, one that arguably represents the heart of the Paris Agreement: Parties can cooperate in many ways, but within a robust system of transparency and robust accounting, possibly with a peer review process associated with it.

4.1.4   Quantity

Limitations on quantity exist in the Kyoto Protocol, both at use as supplementarity, as well as transfer through the Commitment Period Reserve. Neither of these is explicitly present in the Paris Agreement, but there have been many voices asking for such limitations. While the precedent indeed exists in the Kyoto Protocol, it is difficult to point to a "hook" in Article 6 that would justify the operationalization of such restrictions.

Many such quantity restrictions, that do not appear in the text itself, have been suggested by Parties. These limits appear in various forms:

- limits in the issuance of tradable units by Parties, based on a calculation: NDC target multiplied by the NDC period (e.g., 5 years or 10 years);

- limits on the use, with an explicit percentage of NDC compliance, which can be achieved through the use of ITMOs; and

- limits to the transfer itself, including restrictions to avoid speculative trading, or even that there be no secondary trading.

4.1.5   Relationship between Article 6.2 and Article 6.4

A final important consideration for the scope of Article 6.2 in terms of what can be transferred is the relationship between Article 6.2 and Article 6.4.

Article 6.4 produces mitigation outcomes under CMA supervision and modalities and procedures, and it is seen as "issuing" CMA certified mitigation outcomes. The issue can be best described as "does an Article 6.4 mitigation outcome become an ITMO, subject to Article 6.2 rules, at some point following its initial issuance, i.e., in subsequent transfers (e.g., secondary market)?"

Article 6 as the rest of the Paris Agreement is silent on this matter. Two options emerge. One option could be the use of Article 6.2 rules for transfers of Article 6.4 mitigation outcome. Article 6.2 would then become the transfer window for any mitigation outcomes, including emission reductions issued under Article 6.4.

Another option, which seems awkward, would be the creation of parallel transfer rules, to be developed for Article 6.4 mitigation outcomes. Such an option could seem duplicative, and is not justified by any provision in the Paris Agreement. This is not to say that it is not seen as desirable by some, who would prefer not to see fungibility between ITMOs and Article 6.4 mitigation outcomes given the uncertainty over the quality of ITMOs.

The question of issuance itself is implicit. Indeed, where the credit issuance occurs will be crucial to understand when the question of the relationship will arise. One current possibility is for the credit to be issued directly into a UN holding registry. No international transfer would initially take place, and the relationship between Article 6.4 and Article 6.2 would, at least initially, become irrelevant. If secondary transfers are allowed, which is probable, it will have to be decided whether or not this transfer is done under Article 6.2 rules. If so, one should also decide if credits become ITMOs, and if a corresponding adjustment is needed, after the first transfer, from the UN holding registry to another Party's account, or only after the second transfer.

By contrast, if the credit is issued directly in national registries of the host Party, the mitigation outcome would become an ITMO from the first transfer, and the question of the relationship with Article 6.2, with its potential scope-limiting implications, would immediately apply.

4.2   Who Can Transfer?

Eligibility considerations, regarding who can transfer under Article 6.2, could also imply limitations to the scope of Article 6.2.

Submissions refer to a number of participation requirements that may seem innocuous. The first would be to be a Party to the Paris Agreement. This would imply the exclusion of non-Party actors, at least for the issuance and transfer of ITMOs. Non-Parties could not participate unless authorized by a Party. Other limitations include that the Party could be required to have submitted and be maintaining an NDC, as well as having authorized the international transfer of mitigation outcomes.

Less innocuous eligibility considerations could have scope-limiting effects.

Type of nationally determined contribution. This is a first consideration. If a carbon metric was the only acceptable one for ITMOs, and only CO_2e-denominated ITMOs could be transferred, this could lead to limitations to the scope of Article 6.2. Solutions exist, but there are implications, discussed previously. This may lead some to conclude that to be coherent, NDCs would best be expressed in CO_2e budgets.

This view, held by some Parties, would require a Party's commitment to be quantifiable and quantified to participate in Article 6.2 transfers. The imposition of carbon budgets, however, could be seen by some as a step back toward the Kyoto Protocol, and could potentially threaten the "nationally determined" part of NDCs.

Other possible requirements raised by Parties on the type of NDC include having an economy-wide target, the requirement for the NDC to be in multi-year form, or to be expressed in absolute emissions. The implementation of any of these requirements, let alone their combination, would have far reaching implications in terms of the scope of Article 6.2, and the possibility it creates for Parties to meet its NDC through the international transfer of mitigation outcomes.

Regulatory requirements. These are a second consideration. The need for national focal points for Article 6.2, designated national authority (DNA), etc. may emerge as a requirement. Indeed, avoidance of double counting is essential to a well-functioning carbon market, and who will be in charge of accounting, tracking, and reporting has yet to be decided. The task could be the responsibility of a central authority, some CMA-designated body, supervising all transactions. National authorities could directly implement some CMA guidance. Since all Parties participating in the CDM already have a DNA that could undertake this role, these regulatory requirements should not emerge as a major scope-limiting factor.

If baseline-and-crediting approaches are used, the Party could also be required to have a system for setting a baseline in respect of the activity from which the mitigation outcome is issued.

Hardware requirements. These are important for the international transfer of mitigation outcomes and for the avoidance of double counting. Clear data on the amount of units issued, held, and cancelled to achieve NDCs will be needed. Depending on the governance and final outcome of negotiations, this may require the existence of a national registry, potentially connected to an International Transaction Log–like set up. Many submissions highlight that if Parties do not wish or do not have the capacity to establish and maintain a registry, there should exist one under the authority of the UNFCCC secretariat that they can use. The need for a registry should therefore not emerge as a significant limitation to the scope of Article 6.2.

Other requirements. Having an economy-wide long-term low emissions strategy has been mentioned as a potential requirement to participate in the transfer of ITMOs, as well as submitting an indicative emissions trajectory consistent with the long-term targets under this strategy. Submission of a national inventory report could also be a requirement to participate.

5.   Limitations on the Transfer: Accounting

After potential limitations to the nature of mitigation outcomes that may be transferred, and to the eligibility of the Parties involved in transfers, limitations to the transfer itself also have to be considered.

Limitations on the transfer will essentially originate from the accounting guidance, as mandated in Article 6.2 itself and in paragraph 36 of the decision 1/CP.21. This guidance will affect both what can be transferred, and when it can be transferred.

Rules on the timing of the transfer could be impacted by the type of NDCs. Discussions on accounting guidance, especially on corresponding adjustments, have revealed concerns regarding how transfers are recognized and accounted for, as they impact on providing a real picture of what has taken place in relation to the period of the NDC and in meeting the NDC. It may be that, to provide an accurate picture, transfers may need to take place only in certain time windows. While by no means certain, this may also present some limitations of what can be done under Article 6.2.

This accounting guidance may also have to establish the rules for the use of ITMOs for purposes other than meeting a Party's NDC, two of the most pressing cases being the use of ITMOs for non-UNFCCC purposes (e.g. International Civil Aviation Organization), and the cases of voluntary cancellation of ITMOs.

This is important in this context as it would create uncertainty and limit the use of Article 6.2.

ARTICLE 6.4

"A mechanism to contribute to the mitigation of greenhouse gas emissions and support sustainable development is hereby established under the authority and guidance of the Conference of the Parties serving as the meeting of the Parties to this Agreement for use by Parties on a voluntary basis. It shall be supervised by a body designated by the Conference of the Parties serving as the meeting of the Parties to this Agreement, and shall aim:

(a) To promote the mitigation of greenhouse gas emissions while fostering sustainable development;

(b) To incentivize and facilitate participation in the mitigation of greenhouse gas emissions by public and private entities authorized by a Party;

(c) To contribute to the reduction of emission levels in the host Party, which will benefit from mitigation activities resulting in emission reductions that can also be used by another Party to fulfil its nationally determined contribution; and

(d) To deliver an overall mitigation in global emissions."

1. Scope of Article 6.4

Article 6.4 of the Paris Agreement provides the "centralized governance option" for international transfers of mitigation outcomes under Article 6. It establishes a mechanism to be "supervised by a body designated by the Conference of the Parties" and creates a centralized window for Parties to deliver mitigation outcomes that can be used toward their nationally determined contribution (NDC) or transferred to another Party.

For the purposes of this paper, this mechanism will be called A6.4M. Rightfully or wrongfully it is seen by many as the successor in the Paris Agreement of the Clean Development Mechanism (CDM) and it is sometimes also called the sustainable development mechanism, which would imply certain priorities for its activities.

If A6.4M is indeed the successor of the CDM, the procedures and protocols that will be developed for its operationalization may, to some degree, borrow from existing CDM infrastructure and procedures. However, the success of the mechanism in helping achieve the goals of the Paris Agreement will also depend on how much it has learned from the CDM successes, but also for its perceived failures. In this regard, it would also be valuable to look at the experiences from JI.

The scope of Article 6.4 is understood, for the purpose of this paper, to represent what can be done under this article, and who can do it, but also the degree to which it will be used. Defining this scope will require answering questions such as the type of activities covered by the mechanism and the conditions under which actors may take part in it. The answers to such questions, once out in the Conference of the Parties serving as the meeting of the Parties to the Paris Agreement (CMA) decisions, will inevitably limit the scope of Article 6.4.

Such limitations can fall into two categories. Some are explicit, in the sense that they can be found explicitly in the Paris Agreement, or the accompanying 1/CP.21 Decision. Other limitations can be deemed to be implicit, that is, they may be seen as emerging from the interpretation, as well as the impacts of some provisions currently in Article 6.4, or that could emerge from the negotiations of the rulebook for Article 6.4.

2. Explicit Limitations to the Scope of Article 6.4

2.1 Additionality

The term additionality, not present in Article 6.4 itself, appears in the accompanying decision 1/CP.21, paragraph 37.d, which "recommends" that rules, modalities, and procedures be adopted for that article on the basis of "reductions in emissions that are additional to any that would otherwise occur."

How the additionally rules for Article 6.4 will be worded is something that will emerge from negotiations. The degree of stringency will be extremely important as additionality is likely to be one of the most important scope-limiting factors of Article 6.4 in that it will limit the type of activities that will qualify under Article 6.4.

The presence of references to additionality among the elements that will form the basis for the Article 6.4 may indicate that this article may only cover baseline-and-credit approaches. The language of additionality comes from the CDM and directly refers to a baseline-and-credit framework, in which credits are issued by estimating the deviation from a business-as-usual counterfactual. A plausible implication of the additionality clause could therefore be that A6.4M is limited to baseline-and-credit activities. Some more innovative interpretations would see that additionality could also refer to the setting of a baseline in a cap-and-trade, but that would break new ground from a 15-year to 20-year understanding of the meaning of the term "additionality" in the UNFCCC discussions.

An alternative, weaker interpretation of additionality could be of a conditional nature. Indeed, if additionality refers to a baseline-and-credit approach, neither the Paris Agreement nor its accompanying decision explicitly restricts A6.4M activities to baseline-and-credit. The clause could therefore also reasonably be interpreted as imposing additionality if a baseline-and-credit approach is used, but only in that case. Such an interpretation would make the clause a lot less restricting, as it would impose no restriction to activities that are not framed in the baseline-and-credit protocols.

2.2   Sustainable Development

Article 6.4a explicitly states the mechanism shall aim to promote mitigation of emissions "while fostering sustainable development." With sustainable development as one of the first aims of the mechanism, it is very likely that some form of sustainable development certification for projects will emerge.

In the UNFCCC, and the CDM, which the A6.4M is associated with in some ways, there has always been strong resistance to international definitions and guidelines for sustainable development, the Sustainable Development Goals notwithstanding. In current discussions, this continues to be an issue hotly debated, with some Parties making it clear that sustainable development priorities and definitions are a national prerogative.

Nevertheless, the CDM had a Sustainable Development Tool that was made available to be used on a voluntary basis, while the certification for the CDM activities meeting SD goals was done by Parties, through their designated national authority (DNA).

Current discussions on the Paris Agreement are centered very much on transparency, and there is the expectation of a high level of transparency in presenting how the sustainable development conditionality will be met.

While the definition of sustainable development is a national preroragative, the Parties may agree to require reporting not only at the national level, but also at the level of activity. The recent report from ADB on delivering co-benefits for sustainable development through the Future Carbon Fund provides examples of how reporting can be made applying the Agenda 2030 framework.

The modalities for how the sustainable development provision will be met still have to be determined.

It can be expected that some common way of providing "certification" of meeting the sustainable development goal will emerge, and that all Parties will use the same format. It is likely that the entity that would provide such "certification" would be at the Party level, with possibly some guidelines provide by the CMA.

Some Parties have even expressed the view that it is for the Party itself to decide whether or not such a stamp of approval is even required. Assuming certification is indeed required, three potential forms could be envisaged.

- A CDM-type **letter of approval** could be issued, which would be required for a project to qualify for A6.4M crediting.
- A second option could be the setting up of some centralized **guidance with transparency requirements**, setting sustainable development rules that projects would have to respect. Given many Parties view sustainable development as a national prerogative, these rules could refer to the respect of sustainable development norms of the host party, rather than impose a multilateral definition of the term.

- A third, less stringent option would be to establish some **transparency requirement** to participate in A6.4M, but without explicit guidance. The Party or private sector actor involved would merely need to report on its actions.

The form of the certification, its complexity, and its predictability will play an important role whether or not the sustainable development provision will become a limiting factor for the A6.4M. The governance of such "certification," once issued, will also play an important factor in the scope of the A6.4M. Uncertainty and unpredictability could compound the level of complexity. From this point of view the CDM was not seen as making sustainable development mechanism a large barrier—and that was seen as good by market participants, while many in civil society decried the perceived lack of stringency in getting the letter of approval.

Box: Future Carbon Fund–Delivering Co-Benefits for Sustainable Development

The Future Carbon Fund (FCF), a trust fund managed by the Asian Development Bank (ADB) has been supporting Clean Development Mechanism (CDM) projects in the Asia and Pacific region since 2009. The FCF is supporting a diversified portfolio of 36 CDM projects implementing a spectrum of renewable energy, energy efficiency, waste management, and transport sector projects in 12 developing member countries in the region.

Recognizing that the assessment of the delivery of sustainable development co-benefits was not mandated under the CDM and that there has been limited analysis of the project features and circumstances that allow co-benefits to be maximized, ADB has assessed the contribution of the FCF portfolio projects to sustainable development including qualitative and quantitative analysis of the social, environmental, and economic co-benefits that these projects are delivering.

The FCF assessment demonstrates that the FCF portfolio projects are not only reducing 2.95 million tons of carbon dioxide equivalent per annum but are also delivering a broad set of co-benefits to more than 10.5 million people in the region. These include improving energy access and energy security, employment generation, diffusion of low-carbon technologies, technological innovation, health benefits associated with reduction in air pollution, reduced dependence on imported fuels, reduced traffic congestion, and an increase in net trade of technologies and services. The FCF experience demonstrates strong linkages between investments in climate change mitigation projects and the delivery of sustainable development co-benefits.

Article 6.4 of the Paris Agreement provides for a new mechanism by which public and private entities can support greenhouse gas (GHG) emission reductions and sustainable development. The Paris Agreement mentions the intrinsic relationship between sustainable development and climate change actions and has a greater emphasis on sustainable development compared to the Kyoto Protocol.

As the negotiations for establishing a rulebook for Article 6 of the Paris Agreement intensify with targeted finalization before the end of 2018, the assessment and recommendations of the FCF report could be considered in the development of new market mechanisms. In particular, the new mechanism under Article 6.4 may require GHG mitigation projects to demonstrate that they will deliver co-benefits. The delivery of the expected co-benefits could be monitored using a simple methodology based on the Sustainable Development Goals targets. Co-benefits may also be included in the scope of validation and verification which would also help in ensuring much desired transparency in the overall context of the Paris Agreement.

Source: https://www.adb.org/sites/deault/files/publication/389821/future-carbon-fund.pdf.

2.3   Environmental Integrity

Article 6.4 does not explicitly mention ensuring environmental integrity as a goal, but it has to be seen as implied. However, Paragraph 37b of decision 1/CP.21 "recommends" that rules, modalities, and procedures be adopted by the CMA on the basis of "Real, measurable and long-term benefits related to the mitigation of climate change."

Some possible scope limitations are as follows:

- How complex the rules, modalities, and procedures will be to ensure environmental integrity?
- Specific metric tied to the "measurability" requirement (see 3.1)
- Whether or not there will be a compliance check?
- Who checks for compliance—Parties or CMA?

All these elements, depending on how they are implemented, can make the A6.4M a more, or less, attractive instrument to use in meeting the NDCs.

2.4   Authorization

One of the provisions in Article 6.4 is to "incentivize and facilitate private sector involvement." Paragraph 37a of decision 1/CP.21 "recommends" that rules, modalities, and procedures be adopted on the basis of "voluntary participation *authorized* by each Party involved." This paragraph produces a clear limitation to the scope of A6.4M: private sector actors wishing to invest under the A6.4M will be required to obtain authorization from the Party where the mitigation action is located.

What form this authorization will take is yet to be determined. In the CDM, the DNA was responsible for declaring the host country's authorization of the project, in a letter of approval as well as providing authorization from an Annex 1 Party.

As this is the Paris Agreement, and all Parties have obligations, the Annex I/non-Annex I difference will disappear. The complexity of how the authorization for participation will be granted, how and under what conditions it can be withdrawn, will also play an important role of how much the A6.4M will be used.

At its extreme, it may be a blanket approval for private entities to participate in A6.4M activities in a certain jurisdiction. At the other extreme, it may continue to be a project-by-project approval, granted through a complex and uncertain process, with periodic review that is seen, or emerges, as arbitrary.

2.5   Double Counting

Another explicit potential limitation present in the text relates to accounting. Article 6.5 precludes any double counting in the context of the A6.4M. While this seems natural, it may become a limitation depending on how the final interpretation is made in the rulebook for the A6.4M.

In addition, if there is some level of latitude how the double counting provision is to be operationalized, with Parties having some level of latitude within those guidelines, this may also lead to some Parties not finding buyers of mitigation outcomes from the A6.4M. If we are to take this further, a diversity of approaches in addressing double counting may damage the credibility of the A6.4M.

2.6   Overall Mitigation

Limitations to the scope of the article could be understood not only as those regulatory restrictions limiting the type of activities included in the mechanism or the type of Parties eligible to participate, but also elements and conditions restricting the actual use that is made of the mechanism.

In that case, the overall mitigation clause present in Article 6.4.d, stating the mechanism "shall aim...to deliver an overall mitigation in global emissions," may well turn out to be a scope-limiting factor. Many define overall mitigation as having a use of mitigation outcomes toward NDCs that is less than the actual abatement in atmospheric terms. Leaving some of the abatement unused, or uncredited, would thus make the A6.4M a tool to increase ambition.

A first, potentially scope-limiting issue regards the status of this clause. A weak interpretation of the "shall aim" would suggest that delivering overall mitigation would not be obligatory. Achieving overall mitigation would be a general aim of the mechanism—an obligation of conduct and not a result. Parties could participate without being required to deliver overall mitigation, but shall aim to deliver it.

An alternative, stronger interpretation of the "shall aim" could bestow the overall mitigation clause with an obligatory status. Parties must deliver overall mitigation when participating in A6.4M. Such an interpretation could be understood to limit the scope of the article in the sense that it could create important disincentives toward the use of the mechanism, if Parties can only transfer or use a part of the achieved mitigation outcome toward their NDC.

A second issue relates to how overall mitigation is actually delivered. Indeed, how the overall mitigation is achieved, and by who, will affect the level of incentive for Parties to use A6.4M.

One way is through the use of a very conservative baseline. There is indeed some degree of agreement among Parties that business-as-usual baselines, as defined in the CDM, will not be sufficient to reach the objectives of the Paris Agreement.

However, the construction of counterfactuals for baseline-and-crediting already involves a significant amount of uncertainty. Using a conservative baseline would add yet another layer of uncertainty, as the meaning of the word "conservative" is very subjective—subject to the interpretation of every Party. A second option would be to have an objectively defined percentage, inferior to a hundred, which will reflect the amount abated that can be used toward NDCs.

If the second option is preferred, it will have to be decided when the overall mitigation clause is to be applied. There are three options. First, overall mitigation could be *delivered at issuance* itself. Fewer credits would be issued than the abatement that has actually occurred in atmospheric terms.

A second option would be to apply overall mitigation *during the first transfer* to another Party. The host Party would then transfer less than what has actually been issued. If there is indeed a transfer to another party, this second option is very similar to the first.

However, in the case where the host Party does not transfer the credits but uses them toward its own NDC, the first option would deliver overall mitigation whereas the second would not. This second option could therefore create potentially unwelcome distortionary effects, as it would disincentivize the transfer of A6.4M credits and instead encourage their direct use by the host Party.

A third option would be to deliver the overall mitigation *at usage.* The Party using the mitigation outcome, whether it be the host Party directly or after a transfer, could only use toward its NDC only a determined percentage of the A6.4M credits it has at its disposition.

2.7   Share of Proceeds

Article 6.6 clearly states that "a share of proceeds from activities under the mechanism referred to in paragraph 4 of this Article" shall be raised, which shall be used toward covering administrative expenses as well as adaptation for the developing country Parties. Thus, whether or not a share of proceeds shall be levied is not under debate.

A number of issues remain to be solved however, which will, similar to discussions for overall mitigation above, constrict the degree of use of A6.4M. A first issue is the size of the levy raised, which will likely be a certain percentage.

A second issue is the applicability of the share of proceeds clause. Many Parties are of the opinion that the share of proceeds should only be levied once (e.g., at issuance as was the case with CDM, or at the first transfer), while other proponents would also apply it to every subsequent transfer.

In case it would be decided that the share of proceeds would be levied for every transfer, the question whether the levy will be applied at a constant, progressive, or decreasing rate also poses itself, and has been raised by some Parties.

3.   Implicit Limitations and Issues to Be Considered

In addition to the explicit limitations to the scope of Article 6.4, found either in the text of the Paris Agreement or its accompanying decision, a second set of limitations could emerge. The constructive ambiguity that was left in the text to reach the Paris Agreement leaves significant space for discussion and interpretation. Several possible restricting elements, which are implicit or at least not appear textually in the Paris Agreement, could emerge from the coming negotiations, and impose important limits to the scope of Article 6.4.

3.1   Imposition of a (Carbon) Metric

A first limitation could be pursuant to the unit in which A6.4M credits are issued. Given the insistence of some Parties to denominate Article 6.2 internationally transferred mitigation outcomes (ITMOs) in a carbon metric, if it is decided that Article 6.2 should become the transfer window for A6.4M credits, it could be coherent to also issue the credits from that mechanism in ton of carbon dioxide equivalent.

While having many advantages in terms of market liquidity, transparency, and accountability, the imposition of such a carbon metric could be a restriction to the scope of Article 6.4, by discriminating against activities that are harder to quantify in such a metric. It would also require the creation of convertibility factors from other types of mitigation outcome to carbon dioxide equivalent denominated credits, which may also become a politically sensitive exercise.

3.2   Eligibility Criteria

In the Clean Development Mechanism (CDM) and Joint Implementation, there were eligibility criteria that Parties were required to meet in order to participate. To host CDM projects three basic requirements needs to be met:

- Being a Party to the Kyoto Protocol (only developing Parties can host)
- Voluntary Participation
- Establish a Designated National CDM Authority (DNA)

To use certified emission reductions (CERs) generated by CDM projects (or to participate in Joint Implementation), a Party must meet the following additional eligibility requirements:

- a national system for the estimation of anthropogenic emissions by sources and anthropogenic removals by sinks of all greenhouse gases not controlled by the Montreal Protocol in effect,
- a national registry in place,
- required inventory (national inventory report) submitted, and
- supplementarity information on its assigned amount established and submitted.

If the new A6.4M will indeed be the successor of CDM, it is not unlikely that these eligibility requirements will be recycled for deciding who can host and use the new A6.4M projects and products. During negotiations, other possible requirements have also emerged, which, if adopted, might also limit the scope of A6.4M.

3.2.1   Who Can Host Article 6.4 mechanism (A6.4M)?

The architecture of the Kyoto Protocol, and the division it created between Annex I and non-Annex I countries, structured the rules of the CDM. Thus, only non-Annex I countries could host projects, the mechanism being conceived as a way for industrialized countries to participate in the development of these countries by investing in sustainable projects.

This division no longer exists in the Paris Agreement. As the Annex I vs. non-Annex I division disappears, so should the discrimination in hosting: any Party could in theory host a A6.4M project. This does not mean that there will not exist some conditions that Parties must fulfill to participate. Any Party can host projects, but subject to some eligibility criteria that will have to be determined.

At first glance, for Article 6.4. a first possible criterion would be the requirement for the host Parties to have a DNA. The DNA could be in charge of the sustainable development certification. By imposing eligibility conditions on Parties wishing to participate, a DNA requirement could in theory be a scope-limiting factor. It should however pose no real constraints on Parties, given that all Parties participating in the CDM already possess one.

Registry requirements to become a host Party could also emerge, depending on how A6.4M credits are issued. If the credits are issued directly in a multilateral registry, a Party may not necessarily need a separate national registry, unless it wants to transfer-in credits.

In contrast, if the credits are to be issued in the national registry of the host Party, this would logically impose the requirement for a Party to possess such a registry to host A6.4M projects, thus limiting the scope.

Being a Party to the Paris Agreement will likely be another requirement.

There are other eligibility criteria, which are currently present in the Article 6.4 debate in negotiations, and they include:

- has communicated national inventory reports;
- has communicated and is currently maintaining an NDC;
- has a system in place to check for
    » contribution to fostering sustainable development and
    » conformity with Sustainable Development Goals;
- has a system in place to ensure that human rights are not negatively impacted;
- has a system in place to ensure compliance with relevant standards and procedures;
- has fulfilled the requirements on reporting agreed under the transparency framework;
- has a system in place that ensures stakeholder consultation;
- has a system in place to authorize the participation of public or private entities in the mitigation activity;
- has issued credits in a manner that avoids market fluctuations;
- has complied with the qualitative restrictions on transfers, e.g., to address supplementarity or overselling;
- has complied with restrictions on types of transfers;
- has complied with quantitative restrictions on carry-over;
- has complied with restrictions on the use of vintages of emission reductions; and
- has complied with restrictions for sectors with a high degree of uncertainty in emission estimates.

3.2.2   Who Can Use Article 6.4 mechanism (A6.4M) Products?

Under the CDM, just as only non-Annex I countries could host projects, only Annex I countries were able to use the resulting credits, for the simple reason that only these countries had a carbon budget.

In a world no longer structured by this dichotomy, and in which every Party to the Paris Agreement has an NDC it should aim to meet, there is no rationale, and in fact the Paris Agreement text does not have such a restriction on the use of A6.4M credits. We are indeed already seeing some developing countries making use of CERs. There will, however, still likely be some eligibility restrictions for the usage of these credits.

These restrictions on the use of A6.4M credits by Parties are likely to mirror eligibility restrictions on who can host. They could therefore include the requirement for the acquiring Party to have a DNA, a registry, and be a Party to the Paris Agreement. Similar to under the CDM, requirements to have a national system for the estimation of anthropogenic emissions by sources, and to have submitted annually the most recent inventory could be translated for the use of A6.4M credits.

There are other eligibility criteria currently present in the Article 6.4 debate in negotiations, some of which are the same as for hosting Parties, and they include:

- has a system in place to authorize the participation of public and private entities in the mitigation activity;
- has communicated and is currently maintaining an NDC;
- has a system in place to check for
  - » contribution to fostering sustainable development and
  - » conformity with Sustainable Development Goals;
- has a system in place that ensure that human rights are not negatively impacted;
- has fulfilled the requirements on reporting agreed under the transparency framework;
- does not engage in secondary or speculative trading;
- has complied with its supplementarity provisions;
- has complied with the supplementarity rules (use of emission reductions must be supplemental to domestic action);
- has complied with the qualitative restrictions on transfers (e.g., to address supplementarity or overselling);
- has complied with quantitative restrictions on carry-over;
- has complied with restrictions on the use of vintages of emission reductions;
- has complied with restrictions for sectors with a high degree of uncertainty in emission estimates; and
- has not used pre-2020 credits post-2020.

3.4   Projects Outside or Inside the Scope of Nationally Determined Contributions

An important issue for the scope of Article 6.4 is whether or not the mitigation activities must fall within the scope of the host Party's NDC. Although the article itself makes no explicit mention of this, the topic is highly contentious.

The debate is more specifically focused on the transfer of these mitigation outcomes. Prohibiting transfers from sectors outside the scope of NDCs would effectively imply that Parties would have a limited incentive to pursue projects in such sectors, as they could not transfer the credits nor use them toward their own NDC. Allowing such transfers might incentivize Parties to cover these sectors in their NDCs to gain access to the A6.4M mechanism for these sectors.

A6.4M is above all a tool to enable Parties to meet their NDC. Therefore, some Parties strongly oppose allowing mitigation outcomes from a sector outside the scope of a NDC to be transferred internationally under Article 6.

According to them, a Party wishing to transfer a mitigation outcome from such a sector, should first expand the coverage of its NDC to encompass it. Allowing crediting from outside the scope of NDCs could be one less incentive to expand NDC coverage.

This is disagreed by other Parties, who claim that allowing crediting and transfers from outside the scope of NDCs could in fact lead to increases in ambition. NDCs are only intended to be updated every 5 years. Having to wait for a Party to broaden the scope of its NDC to include a particular sector would hinder progress in that sector.

Since an objective of A6.4M is to attract private sector investment, all efforts should be made to facilitate the entry of these private actors into potential projects, without burdening them with the concern of whether or not the project is likely to be included in the NDC in the coming rounds or not. Rather, these Parties claim that the aim should be to create a virtuous circle to increase coverage and ambition. Allowing credits from such sectors to be internationally transferred will encourage investment, bringing in experience, data, and understanding of the mitigation potentials in these sectors. This is likely to encourage the Party to broaden the scope of its NDC in the following round, eventually toward an economy-wide NDC.

Such transfers from outside the scope of an NDC have also raised double counting concerns. However, at least in the initial transfer, no double counting should occur, as the mitigation outcome could only be counted toward the NDC of the receiving country. No corresponding adjustment would thus have to be carried out. The moment when double counting could potentially occur is if the host Party, encouraged by that sector's momentum, enlarges the scope of its NDC to encompass it. It is then that, if host Party tries to use the mitigation that was already counted toward the receiving party's NDC, double counting could occur. Article 6.5 should in theory preclude such a situation from arising.

3.7   Relationship between Article 6.2 and Article 6.4

It is the view of some Parties that the question of the relationship between Article 6.4 and Article 6.2 can be framed in terms of responsibility. Any activity falling under the scope of Article 6.2 engages the responsibility only of the Parties involved in the transfer, whereas Article 6.4, as a centralized mechanism, involves a globally shared responsibility for transparency and accountability. However, beyond the issue of responsibility, the question of the relationship between these two articles really concerns the conditions under which A6.4M credits can be transferred. If secondary transfers of these credits can indeed occur, the framework for these transfers will have to be determined.

The question hinges on the fungibility of A6.4M credits and ITMOs. Some Parties view Article 6.2 as the transfer window for any mitigation outcome, including those generated under A6.4M.

In their view, A6.4M credits, once transferred, are one type of ITMOs among others, and a corresponding adjustment will be done under the guidance to be developed for Article 6.2.

Some Parties view the two articles as distinct. Due to the existing uncertainty over the quality of ITMOs, some would rather have A6.4M credits kept separate to preserve their integrity. Under this view, a separate window for the transfer of these credits would have to be established, and A6.4M credits would never become ITMOs. The only scope-limiting elements under such a scenario would be those emerging from these separate transfer rules.

ARTICLE 6.2

"Parties shall, where engaging on a voluntary basis in cooperative approaches that involve the use of internationally transferred mitigation outcomes towards nationally determined contributions, promote sustainable development and ensure environmental integrity and transparency, including in governance, and shall apply robust accounting to ensure, inter alia, the avoidance of double counting, consistent with guidance adopted by the Conference of the Parties serving as the meeting of the Parties to this Agreement."

ARTICLE 6.4

"A mechanism to contribute to the mitigation of greenhouse gas emissions and support sustainable development is hereby established under the authority and guidance of the Conference of the Parties serving as the meeting of the Parties to this Agreement for use by Parties on a voluntary basis. It shall be supervised by a body designated by the Conference of the Parties serving as the meeting of the Parties to this Agreement, and shall aim:

(a) *To promote the mitigation of greenhouse gas emissions while fostering sustainable development;*

(b) *To incentivize and facilitate participation in the mitigation of greenhouse gas emissions by public and private entities authorized by a Party;*

(c) *To contribute to the reduction of emission levels in the host Party, which will benefit from mitigation activities resulting in emission reductions that can also be used by another Party to fulfil its nationally determined contribution; and*

(d) *To deliver an overall mitigation in global emissions."*

Article 6.2 of the Paris Agreement recognizes the ability for Parties to engage in voluntary cooperation, which involves the internationally transferred mitigation outcomes (ITMOs) for implementation of their nationally determined contributions (NDCs). The article introduces caveats to these transfers— "shall provisions." One of these provisions, which states that Parties shall apply robust accounting, is yet to be defined.

Under Article 6.2 of the Paris Agreement, a work program is defined to operationalize the accounting provision. Decision 1/CP.21, paragraph 36, requests the Subsidiary Body for Scientific and Technological Advice (SBSTA) to "develop and recommend the guidance referred to under Article 6, paragraph 2." In respect of accounting, "guidance should ensure that double counting is avoided on the basis of a corresponding adjustment by Parties for both anthropogenic emissions by sources and removals by sinks covered by their nationally determined contributions under the Agreement."

Even if corresponding adjustments are referenced in relation to Article 6.2 only, as the discussion around the scope of Article 6.2 and its relationship with Article 6.4 has indicated, corresponding adjustments will also need to be considered in the case of Article 6.4, both when the initial mitigation outcome is created, as well as at further transfers.

This paper seeks to discuss several pertinent issues, which include, in the case of the transfer of a mitigation outcome:

1) defining corresponding adjustments,
2) what is being adjusted,
3) timing of the corresponding adjustment,
4) how to address adjusting for ITMOs originating inside and outside the scope of the NDC,
5) corresponding adjustments with single year NDCs, and
6) corresponding adjustments under Article 6.4.

1.   Defining a Corresponding Adjustment

Article 6.2 of the Paris Agreement, as well as paragraph 36 of Decision 1/CP.21, are unclear when reference is made to a corresponding adjustment. The lack of clarity relates to what is being adjusted and at what time. As such, a number of ways to interpret these provisions are emerging, as well as solutions for the guidance document that is mandated in Decision 1/CP.21.

One way to interpret this is that there are four types of Parties:

- **Acquiring party.** A Party that is participating in a Cooperative Approach, who receives by way of transferring in of an ITMO from another participating Party and who may or may not also be the Using Party.
- **Using party.** A Party that is participating in a Cooperative Approach who has received the ITMO, accounted for the receipt in line with the accounting guidance under Article 6.2, and applied it toward its NDC.
- **Issuing party.** A Party that is participating in a Cooperative Approach, in whose jurisdiction the mitigation action or avoidance of greenhouse gas emissions, etc. has occurred.
- **Transferring party.** A Party that is participating in a Cooperative Approach and transfers out an ITMO to an Acquiring Party, for potential use toward its NDC. For the avoidance of doubt with respect to the very first international transfer of an ITMO, the Issuing Party is also the first Transferring Party.

One approach would envisage that there is a corresponding adjustment only at the beginning by the Issuing Party and the end of the transfer chain by the Using Party respectively, for the purposes of NDC accounting. Even if there is a very long chain of transfers, the only corresponding adjustment that will happen is at issuance and usage. In this interpretation, international transfers do not trigger a corresponding adjustment. The only corresponding adjustment is the one for NDC accounting purposes, which is done at the time of usage of the ITMO by the Using Party toward its NDC.

There are a number of problems with this approach. Although it is an option that needs to be considered, this approach does not appear to make the most sense. If the Issuing Party transfers ITMOs, it does not have the benefit of the mitigation outcome anymore. This needs to be reflected in its NDC accounting. To have them available for use toward its NDC, it would need to reacquire them, even if the Party that holds them did not use them at the end of the NDC period.

Corresponding adjustments made only for use may leave a lack of clarity on the status of the ITMOs in the hands of the Acquiring Parties and Transferring Parties (i.e., within the chain of transfers arising between the Issuing Party and Using Parties).

Figure 1: Corresponding Adjustments and Accounting Using the Nationally Determined Contributions-Based Approach

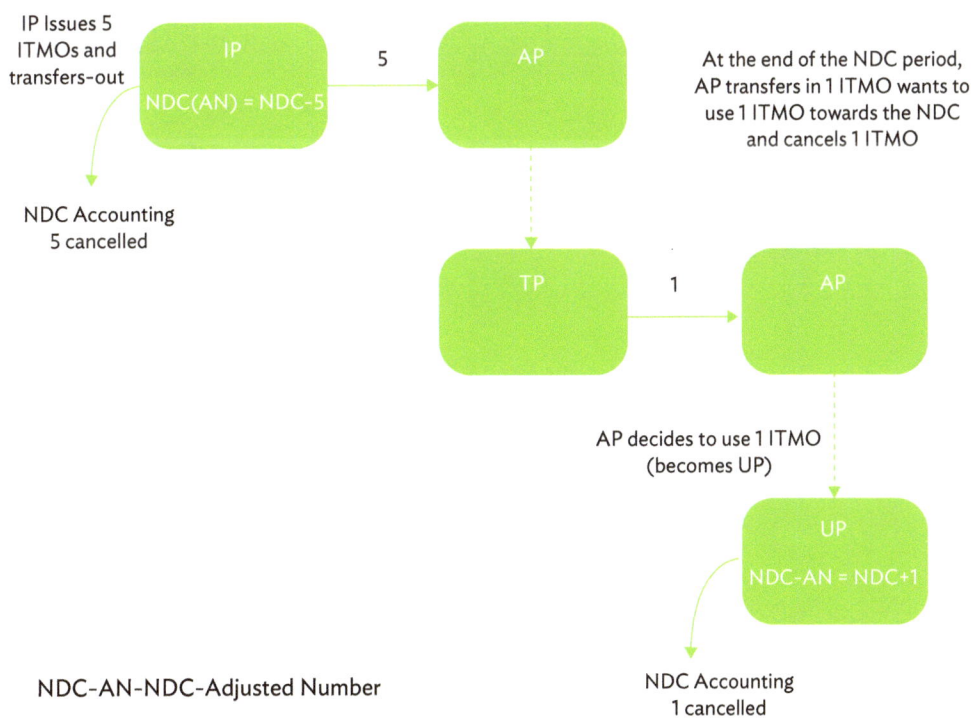

AP = acquiring party, IP = issuing party, ITMO = internationally transferred mitigation outcome, NDC = nationally determined contribution, UP = using party.

Note: Corresponding adjustments only for NDC accounting only at time of ITMO usage toward the NDC.

Source: Technical Support Facility.

However, this scenario and approach poses challenges, including the uncertainty on the Issuing Party (i.e., who cannot use it as it is already transferred) and if it can use the mitigation outcome toward its NDC or if some Using Party, down the transfer chain, will use it at the time of NDC true up.

An alternative approach would support a corresponding adjustment as related to the transfer of mitigation outcome, and that a number, which is the net result of this corresponding adjustment, is then used for NDC accounting. Therefore, a corresponding adjustment occurs every time there is a transfer between Parties (whether Issuing Party, Acquiring Party, Transferring Party, or Using Party).

For example, in a Target (Budget) based approach, the NDC Adjusted number (NDC-AN) = NDC +/- number of ITMOs. Subsequently, the NDC accounting takes place at the end of the NDC period, which uses corresponding adjustments for the purpose of the NDC accounting.

Figure 2: Corresponding Adjustments and Accounting Using the Nationally Determined Contribution-Based Approach

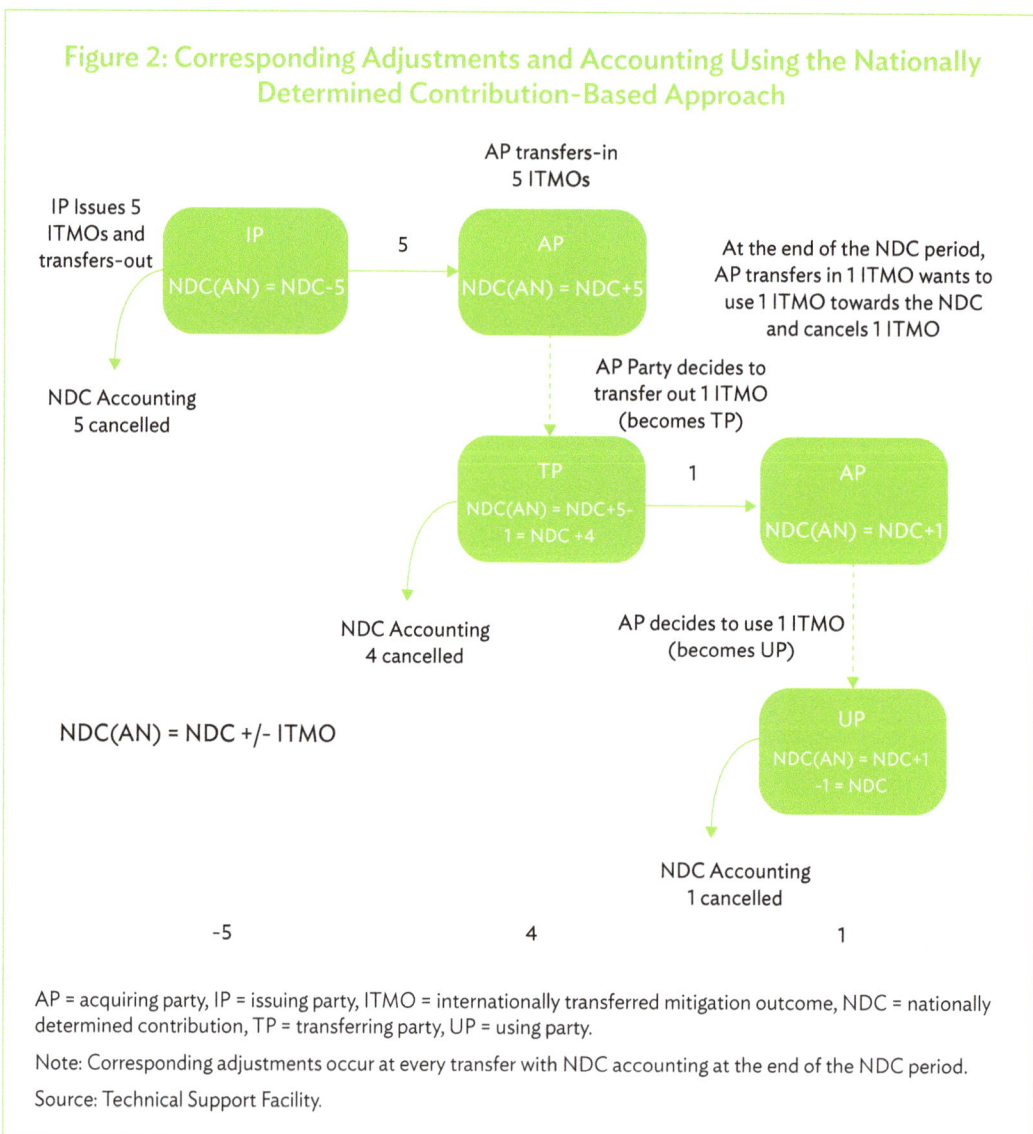

AP = acquiring party, IP = issuing party, ITMO = internationally transferred mitigation outcome, NDC = nationally determined contribution, TP = transferring party, UP = using party.

Note: Corresponding adjustments occur at every transfer with NDC accounting at the end of the NDC period.

Source: Technical Support Facility.

In this scenario, the Issuing Party carries out a corresponding adjustment at issuance, which is then seen as part of the NDC accounting, which takes place at the end of the period for the Issuing Party. There is a corresponding adjustment for NDC accounting that takes place at the time of usage by the Using Party toward its NDC, at the end of the NDC period.

In this scenario, it is clear that the Issuing Party no longer has access to the mitigation outcome that it has issued and transferred.

2.   What Is Being Adjusted?

The question of what is being adjusted has presented four different options:

- target-based approach
- emission-based approach
- buffer registry-based approach
- emission reduction-based approach

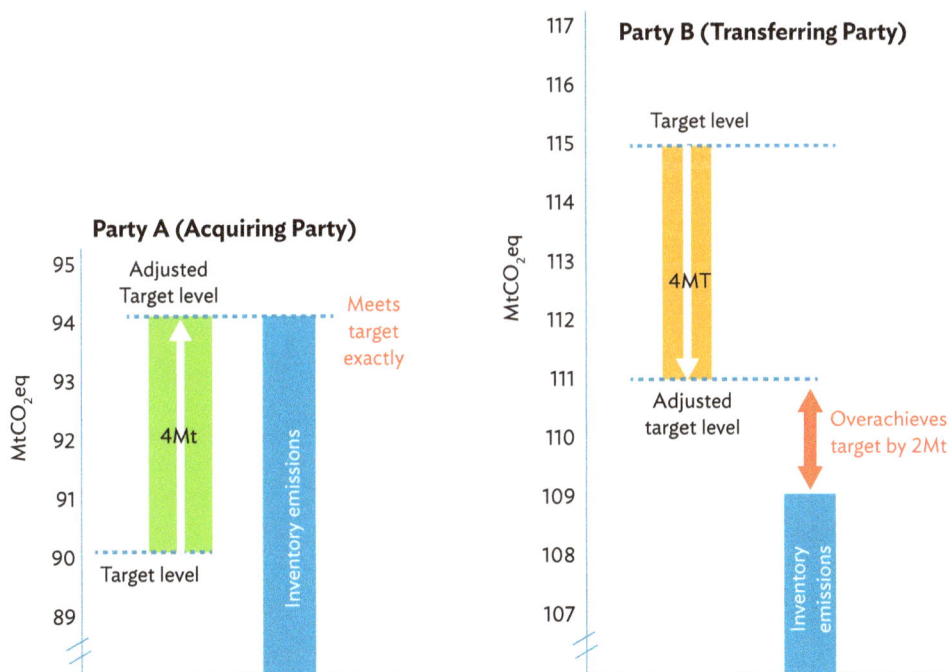

Figure 3: Corresponding Adjustments Using a Target-Based Approach

Mt = Metric ton, MtCO$_2$e = metric tons of carbon dioxide equivalent.

Source: C. Hood. Presentation at Workshop on "Corresponding Adjustment" as part of Article 6 accounting Ottawa, Canada, 20 February 2017.

Target-based approach. The target-based approach relies on using the NDC as a starting point (Figure 3). However, what is being adjusted is not the NDC itself, but a number that uses the NDC as a starting point but is different from the NDC. This can be referred to as the NDC Adjusted Number (NDC-AN). The Issuing or Transferring Party would subtract the ITMO from their NDC-AN while the acquiring country would add the ITMO to their NDC-AN.

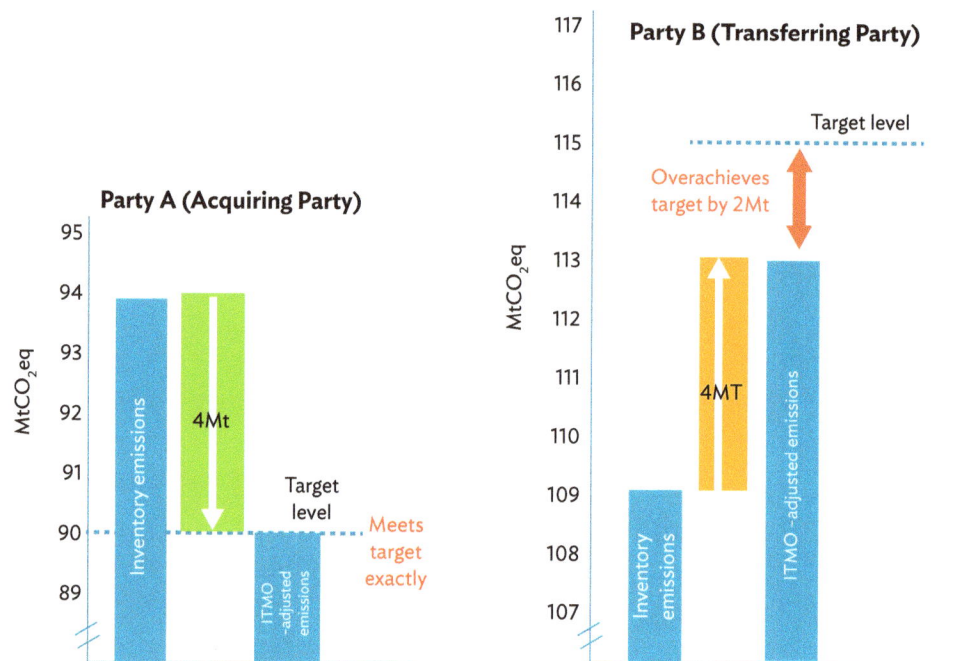

Figure 4: Corresponding Adjustments Using an Inventory-Based Approach

ITMO = internationally transferred mitigation outcome, Mt = Metric ton, MtCO$_2$e = metric tons of carbon dioxide equivalent.

Source: C. Hood. Presentation at Workshop on "Corresponding Adjustment" as part of Article 6 accounting Ottawa, Canada, 20 February 2017.

Emissions-based approach. For the emissions-based approach (Figure 4), the focus is on the adjustment of the inventory. Again, a new number, referred to as an accounting balance or ITMO adjusted emissions using the inventory as a starting point, is created and then adjusted, based on in/out transfers in the NDC period. The inventory itself is not adjusted. The Transferring Party would apply an addition and the acquiring party a subtraction.

Buffer registry account-based approach. The third approach involves the creation of a buffer registry. Beginning from zero, it would count transfers in and out and produce a net total. This value, together with the Inventory and the NDC number, could give a picture of how the Party is performing vs. its NDC pledge.

Emission reduction-based approach. The emission reduction approach involves the calculation of emissions reductions required to achieve the NDC. A subtraction would be applied to the Issuing Party and an addition to the acquiring party.

Each approach has its relative benefits and caveats. The target approach and creation of a budget can be seen as a way to simplify the adjustment process, by creating units within a budget. While this is plausible, the creation of a budget would run counter to the bottom-up principle of the Paris Agreement. The adjustment of targets may place a significant burden on the political system as it may be difficult to cope with continuously moving targets. The method selected should also take into consideration the setting of future NDCs. If a target is to be adjusted, this could affect the setting of future NDCs and the expected future increase in the level of ambition of the NDC.

The inventory approach is largely considered beneficial due to its simplicity. The approach is traceable, transparent, and better in an environmental integrity sense, given the basis for adjustment is from a real number—the inventory emissions, albeit not the actual inventory, which is considered sacrosanct and should give a picture of total emissions both at a national and global stocktake level. Inventories are a well-understood number, and something that Parties and stakeholders can refer to.

The use of an inventory approach creates an incentive for Parties to improve their inventory to allow them to engage in transfers.

The buffer registry approach has advantages in that it separates the accounting from the two numbers that should not change: the inventory and NDC. In addition, it recognizes the uncertainty associated with how and when transfers are put to use. The adjustments are done to an account every time there is a transfer, and that is noncontroversial. In the case of the two other approaches, since they are numbers with a specific meaning, there is an on-going debate as to how the ITMOs are used, and how that influences the adjustment to the two numbers. Some may see this approach not as approach on its own, but as a simple intermediate step in the target and inventory approach.

The emission reduction approach is the reverse to the target approach in that it is an adjustment of what is required to achieve the NDC instead of adjusting the NDC (NDC-AN). However, perhaps it would over complicate the adjustment process since an emission reduction number needs to be created and then adjusted. It would be simpler to the use the NDC-AN.

A few summary points are particularly relevant. Whichever approach is selected, guidance could indicate one synchronous approach for all. However, the other option is that Parties choose their own method and apply this method consistently or the same method applies to all Parties.

3.   Basis and Timing of Corresponding Adjustment

Regardless of which method or approach to the adjustment is chosen, there remains a question whether the corresponding adjustment is applied at

- the time of transfer where adjustment by Transferring Party is made upon transfer from Transferring or Issuing Party to Acquiring Party,
- the time of usage toward NDC where adjustment is done upon usage or cancellation by the Acquiring Party,
- the time of acquisition where adjustment by Acquiring Party is made upon its acquisition from Transferring or Issuing Party, and
- the time of submitting information as in Article 13.7.

One view is to propose that the adjustment ought to reflect what is happening—the transfer. The adjustment at transfer simplifies the approach and assures the adjustment is corresponding. If the option of adjusting at the time of usage is employed, then the Transferring Party would be uncertain about achieving their NDC, because they must wait on another Party to use or not use an ITMO. However, this implies that the requirement for accounting toward the NDC of the ITMO remains with the Issuing Party until usage.

There are concerns that if the acquiring party adjusts only for what is being used, then there may be unused transfers, and this may present transparency concerns.

4.   Adjusting for the International Transfer of Mitigation Outcomes Originating Inside and Outside the Scope of the Nationally Determined Contribution

Paragraph 36 of Decision 1/CP.21 states that corresponding adjustments are applied for emissions covered by the NDC. This would appear to rule out any possibility of transfers from outside the scope of the NDC. However, the discussion still needs to clarify this.

Four possible scenarios could occur when considering ITMOs originating inside or outside the NDC scope:

- inside to inside NDC,
- inside to outside NDC,
- outside to inside NDC, and
- outside to outside NDC.

For the scenarios that cover transfers outside the scope of the NDC, it is not clear how an adjustment can be applied. If a transfer was made from outside the NDC, what adjustment would be applied? Furthermore, it is contended that transfers from outside the NDC to inside would dilute an NDC. As the aim of the Paris Agreement is to increase ambition this would not be beneficial.

For these reasons, an approach can be proposed to mitigate these concerns. Transfers would be separated for those within the NDC and those outside. Accounting for transfers outside the NDC may aid capacity building in accounting and adds further transparency regarding transfers.

If guidance allows mitigation outcomes to be created outside the NDC, there are two options for applying a corresponding adjustment. The first would be a Party applies a corresponding adjustment for all ITMOs created upon international transfer and the second option is that a corresponding adjustment is only applied to those created inside the NDC, upon international transfer.

If guidance were to dictate that mitigation outcomes can only be created inside the NDC the situation is simplified somewhat. The Party would always be required to apply a corresponding adjustment upon international transfer.

5. Corresponding Adjustments with Single Year Nationally Determined Contributions

Many Parties have single year NDCs. This presents a problem for accounting for international transfers, as there is existing uncertainty over the emissions pathway in nontarget years. The issue of transparency, accuracy, completeness, comparability, and consistency in the context of single year targets is complex and has been elaborated at length in research. It is however important to mention that the use of single year targets creates a lot of complexities in conjunction with Article 6. Depending on the timing of the adjustment, one could reach very different outcomes in accounting for and achieving their NDC.

Several options in the Informal Note are discussed as a method to mitigate the challenge of corresponding adjustments with single year targets and are listed below:

- There is no specific guidance for single year targets.
- The representative transfer of ITMOs over the NDC period is accounted in the target year.
- The use of ITMOs in each period is reflected in the biennial reports under Article 13.7.

Using Party

- The use of ITMOs is limited to those with the same vintage as the NDC target year.
- The use of ITMOs is compared to an emissions trajectory throughout the NDC implementation period.
- The numbers used would be the average of ITMO acquisitions, or average ITMO use, over the NDC implementation period in the NDC target year.
- The use of acquisitions or average ITMO use over the period of the activity is accounted in the NDC target year.

Transferring Party

- The international transfer of ITMOs is limited to mitigation in the NDC target year (i.e., vintage limit).
- The numbers used would be the international transfer of ITMOs outside the NDC target year, with no corresponding adjustment.
- The international transfer of ITMOs is compared to an emissions trajectory throughout the NDC implementation period.
- The average international transfer of ITMOs over the NDC implementation period is applied in the NDC target year.
- The use of average ITMOs created, issued, or transferred over the period of the activity is accounted in the NDC target year (ITMO accounted in target year equals ITMO generated by the activity divided by number of years in period of the activity).

To account only in the target year would show a representative picture of ITMO activity with respect to strict NDC achievement but may show an inaccurate picture of overall Party behavior throughout the NDC period. For example, if a Party only engages in an international transfer in the single target year, the Parties may show they achieve the target but the activity over the other years is not considered. To rectify this, the activity could be averaged or linearized, or the NDC could be converted into a budget and trajectory. Yet, this would be counter to the bottom-up process of the Paris Agreement and could "force" a reformulation of party's NDCs.

Using an average or linear approach, the ITMO activity in the target year would be more representative of the on-going party activity and consequently enhance environmental integrity. While it would meet the requirements of Article 6 for environmental integrity, it would not be considered robust accounting given that it may not be precise to the last ton.

6.   Corresponding Adjustments under Article 6.4

Article 6 is not explicit on the relationship between Articles 6.2 and 6.4. The relationship will influence if credits from A6.4M are subject to corresponding adjustments, and if so, when. Three options for the relationship of Article 6.4 credits and ITMOs prevail.

If Article 6.4 credits were seen to be treated as ITMOs all the time, Parties would follow the guidance determined for ITMOs under Article 6.2 and apply corresponding adjustment as in Article 6.2.

Alternatively, if credits are not ITMOs all the time, a parallel set of rules could be created exclusive to Articles 6.4 and 6.2 guidance would not apply. However, Article 6.4 rules may still indicate the necessity for corresponding adjustment.

A third option is possible where Article 6.4 credits become ITMOs at some point. This is where significant discussion persists.

When credits are created and issued into a UN holding registry they are not ITMOs, as no international transfer has occurred, and subsequently no corresponding adjustment is required. However, If the credit is then transferred out of the holding registry to a Party's account, views diverge.

The first view is that this transfer to a Party's account is an international transfer and thus a corresponding adjustment is required. This would ensure that there is no double counting as Parties respectively do a subtraction and addition from their accounts.

A second view does not consider the transfer from holding registry to a Party's account as an international transfer. The outcome of this view is that no corresponding adjustment would be necessary. However, this may produce a risk of double counting as the ITMO is not adjusted by the Transferring Party but there would be an adjustment by the Acquiring Party.

Considerations on the Scope of Article 6.8

ARTICLE 6.8

"Parties recognize the importance of integrated, holistic and balanced non-market approaches being available to Parties to assist in the implementation of their nationally determined contributions, in the context of sustainable development and poverty eradication, in a coordinated and effective manner, including through, inter alia, mitigation, adaptation, finance, technology transfer and capacity-building, as appropriate. These approaches shall aim to: (a) Promote mitigation and adaptation ambition; (b) Enhance public and private sector participation in the implementation of nationally determined contributions; and (c) Enable opportunities for coordination across instruments and relevant institutional arrangements."

ARTICLE 6.9

"A framework for non-market approaches to sustainable development is hereby defined to promote the non-market approaches referred to in paragraph 8 of this Article."

The third part of Article 6 concerns the establishment of a framework for non-market approaches. It is still largely unclear what will be covered under this framework, but some focus is starting to emerge. Article 6.8 recognizes the importance of integrated, holistic, and balanced non-market approaches and Article 6.9 defines a framework for these approaches.

1. Key issues

The introduction of a framework for non-market approaches (NMA) reflects that some Parties see the United Nations Framework Convention on Climate Change (UNFCCC) as based on non-market principles and that the emphasis should be on non-market approaches. The NMA was introduced alongside the discussions that took place in relation to a Framework for Various Approaches and the New Market-Based Mechanism. The negotiation process at the early stages as well as today is characterized by the expectation that progress should be made on all items under Article 6 more or less simultaneously.

This part of Article 6 is different from Article 6.2 and Article 6.4 in that a work program has to be decided instead of guidance notes, rules, modalities, or procedures. The similarity with these articles is that Article 6.8 is also aiming at assisting in the implementation of the nationally determined contributions (NDCs).

2.   Scope of the Framework

Article 6.9 states "A framework for non-market approaches to sustainable development is hereby defined to promote the non-market approaches referred to in paragraph 8 of this Article." There are two, maybe not mutually exclusive, major views on the role of a framework for NMAs:

(i)   The framework should provide for sharing experience and best practices.

(ii)   The framework should provide for enhanced support to developing countries through finance and capacity-building for the implementation of NMAs. This would also include contributing to mapping and registering needs of countries and helping match them with means of implementation.

Some Parties stress the synergetic element in Article 6.8 and propose that success stories could be identified and reported. According to this view, the role of the framework would be to facilitate both the identification of synergetic approaches and to ensure that Parties can take stock of them. For some Parties, this can be done using the existing institutions under the UNFCCC, and reporting could be made in accordance with Article 13.

The second view is more directed to providing financial support to NMAs. This requires, for instance, having a clear definition of the scope and modalities within which the developed countries would support the developing country in accessing the means of implementation in a coordinated manner so the country could fulfill its climate change commitments. For this purpose, some Parties also propose that they establish a registry of needs to implement their NDCs through NMAs, complemented by a matching facility that ensures the articulation between the needs and the means of implementation regarding the support on finance, technology transfer, and capacity building.

3.   Scope of Non-Market Approaches

There are not many clear concepts of what could constitute a NMA. The list of principles proposed by the Parties that would guide what NMAs could be is quite long. These principles are based on different articles of the Paris Agreement, illustrating that the Parties view the role of NMAs differently. Following references made by Parties generally to the Paris Agreement, NMAs should

- contribute to the objectives of the Paris Agreement referred to in its Article 2;
- not infringe human rights and other rights;
- provide incentives for progression beyond participating Parties' then current NDCs pursuant to Article 4, paragraph 3;
- maintain harmony among environmental, social, and economic dimensions of sustainable development, taking into consideration Article 4, paragraphs 7 and 15;
- ensure that the NMAs do not duplicate work under the Convention, the Kyoto Protocol, the Paris Agreement, or other multilateral forums;

- not be reliant on market-based approaches but may provide incentives for domestic mitigation actions in the form of payments without transfer of units;
- ensure manageable sustainable development transition for all Parties; and
- avoid unilateral measures and employ non-discriminatory practices.

As part of Article 6, the Parties suggest that NMAs should

- be voluntary;
- allow for higher adaptation and mitigation ambition;
- promote environmental integrity; and
- assist participating Parties in implementing the objectives of their NDCs.

Referring specifically to Article 6.8–6.9, the Parties suggest that NMAs

- are integrated, holistic, and balanced and are to assist in the implementation of NDCs;
- promote sustainable development and poverty eradication;
- promote mitigation and adaptation ambition;
- enhance public and private sector participation in the implementation of NDCs; and
- aim to enable opportunities for coordination across instruments and relevant institutional arrangements.
- could include a specific mechanism for the creation of Adaptation Benefit Units.

4.   Scope of Work Program

The type of activities that could be included is typically presented in the form of examples by Parties and not given any definition. The work program stipulated in decision 40 of the Paris Agreement, should consider how to

(i)   enhance linkages and create synergy between, mitigation, adaptation, finance, technology transfer and capacity-building, among others and

(ii)   facilitate the implementation and coordination of NMAs.

The decision for a work program does not contain a mandate to define NMAs, only to consider linkages and to facilitate implementation and coordination. However, it is likely that further specifications, both in terms of what they are and what they are not, may enter into the decision on the work program.

Some Parties suggest that the work program focus on thematic areas identified by the Parties. Some Parties list suggestions for the type of areas or approaches that could be relevant. Such areas and approaches could be

- the reduction, removal, or reform of fossil fuel subsidies;
- the increase of deployment of renewable energy technologies in power generation;
- the phase out of inefficient and polluting technologies;

- the introduction of carbon taxes, ecolabelling, and other technical standards;
- the implementation of training and education programs; and
- support to research and development.

One suggestion is that the work program should not be an international endeavor but that each Party should develop a work program and possibly include this in their biennial reports.

5.   Governance

The views on governance follow the expectations on what the role of the framework will be. Many Parties stress the need to avoid duplication and to use what is already developed under the UNFCCC, while others suggest new forums for the framework.

One view is that the Subsidiary Body for Scientific and Technological Advice (SBSTA) should implement the framework and the work program during or in connection with its regular meetings.

Another proposal is to establish a task force, to be convened by the Chair of the SBSTA. This task force would meet regularly and consist of representatives from the Parties, but also possibly including members from social organizations, the Green Climate Fund, the Technology Executive Committee, and the Paris Committee on Capacity-building.

A third option is to create a Permanent Forum, also held in conjunction with SBSTA meetings.

A fourth proposal suggests using existing committees and structures (e.g., Adaptation Fund, Standing Committee on Finance) with or without expansion of their terms of reference. These existing bodies would implement activities relevant to the work program.

There is also another proposal for a Committee for the Future.

There are additional proposals such as leaving the governance structures to the Parties and giving SBSTA and the Subsidiary Body for Implementation a coordinating role in implementing the framework.

One proposal includes the idea that the technical examination process on mitigation (following decision 110 of 1/CP.21) and on adaptation (following decision 125 of 1/CP.21) could be under the framework of NMAs. The Party suggesting this argues that the technical examination process and technical expert meetings are established processes for considering policy approaches that fit well with the purposes of Article 6.8.

Transparency, Reporting, and Review Provisions Related to Article 6 of the Paris Agreement

Background

The operationalization of the Paris Agreement depends on the Conference of the Parties serving as the meeting of the Parties to the Paris Agreement (CMA) decisions ("Paris Rulebook") to be taken on several provisions established by different articles. Some of these provisions have potential inter-linkages, i.e., decisions taken in relation to one article may affect decisions to be taken in relation to another article and vice versa.

This is particularly relevant for reporting and reviewing requirements of information submitted under Article 13 of the Paris Agreement ("Transparency Framework"), including information related to the use of Article 6, paragraph 2 ("Cooperative Approaches") and Article 6, paragraph 4 ("Mechanism to contribute to the mitigation of greenhouse gas emissions and support sustainable development").

1. The Transparency Framework of the Paris Agreement

Article 13 of the Paris Agreement established an enhanced transparency framework for action and support (Transparency Framework),[2] with the purpose, among others, of providing a clear understanding of climate change action, including clarity of progress toward achieving Parties' individual nationally determined contributions (NDC) under Article 4.[3]

As part of the requirements of the Transparency Framework, all Parties of the Paris Agreement will have to submit biennial transparency reports[4] that will be subject to a technical expert review (TER).[5] In addition, each Party shall participate in a facilitative,

---

[2] UNFCCC. 2015. *Paris Agreement*. Article 13, Paragraph 1. https://unfccc.int/sites/default/files/english_paris_agreement.pdf.

[3] UNFCCC. 2015. *Paris Agreement*. Article 13, Paragraph 5.https://unfccc.int/sites/default/files/english_paris_agreement.pdf.

[4] UNFCCC. 2016. *Decisions Adopted by the Conference of the Parties*. Paragraph 90. https://unfccc.int/resource/docs/2015/cop21/eng/10a01.pdf.

[5] UNFCCC. 2015. *Paris Agreement*. Article 13, Paragraph 11. https://unfccc.int/sites/default/files/english_paris_agreement.pdf.

multilateral consideration of progress (FMCP) with respect to efforts under Article 9, and its respective implementation and achievement of its NDC.[6]

The modalities, procedures, and guidelines (MPG) of the Transparency Framework, including the TER and FMCP, are being negotiated under the Ad Hoc Working Group for the Paris Agreement (APA). In the latest negotiation round,[7] an informal note by the co-facilitators was produced, with possible elements to be considered under possible headings and subheadings of the MPG.[8]

2.   Transparency, Reporting, and Review Provisions Related to Article 6

A particular reporting requirement of the Transparency Framework that is relevant for Article 6.2 and Article 6.4 is the "information necessary to track progress made in implementing and achieving its nationally determined contribution under Article 4."[9]

When a Party decides to engage on a voluntary basis in Cooperative Approaches toward NDC or benefit from mitigation activities resulting from the A6.4M, it can be assumed that specific and additional information related to the Cooperative Approach and the mechanism will be part of the "information necessary to track progress." This information is to be submitted through biennial transparency reports and "shall undergo a technical expert review" and will be presented and discussed during the facilitative, multilateral consideration of progress.

It is important to highlight that specific and additional information will only be required for those Parties that are engaged in the "Cooperative Approaches" and/or the mechanism. Other Parties will only have to submit information necessary to track progress made in implementing and achieving the NDC. In other words, there are two layers of information to be submitted. One layer regards the information necessary to track progress in implementing and achieving the NDC. The second layer will be information required to track internationally transferred mitigation outcomes (ITMOs)under Article 6.2 and transfers under Article 6.4.

---

[6]   Footnote 4.
[7]   Resumed session of the APA held on 7–15 November 2017 in conjunction with the 47th sessions of the subsidiary bodies in Bonn, Germany from 6–15 November 2017.
[8]   UNFCCC. 2017. *Draft Elements for APA Agenda Item 5.* http://unfccc.int/files/meetings/bonn_nov_2017/in-session/application/pdf/apa_5_informal_note_.pdf.
[9]   UNFCCC. 2015. *Paris Agreement.* Article 13, Paragraph 7.b.https://unfccc.int/sites/default/files/english_paris_agreement.pdf.

3. The Inter-Linkages among Different Negotiations Agenda Items

The information to be reported, and therefore to be reviewed, is yet to be decided as part of the "Paris Rulebook," i.e., the set of CMA decisions to be taken in December 2018. The guidance on Cooperative Approach is being negotiated under the Subsidiary Body for Scientific and Technological Advice (SBSTA) agenda item 11(a) and the rules, modalities, and procedures for the mechanism under 11(b), while the MPG of the Transparency Framework are being negotiated under APA agenda item 5. In addition, there is also the guidance for accounting for Parties' NDC, as referred to in Article 4, paragraph 13, being negotiated under APA agenda item 3c.

The SBSTA informal note by the co-chairs on draft elements for guidance on Cooperative Approach have listed possible elements on reporting that can be organized according to the role each Party has in the Cooperative Approach.

During the APA sessions it was recognized that there are inter-linkages among the different agenda items under negotiation[10] and that "transparency negotiators" do not have all the necessary expertise and/or information in hand to define in details the reporting and review requirements necessary to all provisions of the Paris Agreement. Therefore, "placeholders" were included in the informal note on the development of the MPG of the Transparency Framework, including in the list of possible elements for information related to Article 6.

Based on the use of "placeholders," it could be expected that in the case of Article 6, the SBSTA agenda items should conclude its work in a timely manner to inform the relevant APA agenda items. However, as can be noted, there is still a lack of clarity and differences in what are supposed to be reported according to SBSTA and APA informal notes. The fact that both negotiation tracks occur in parallel and have the same deadline (i.e., December 2018) adds an additional level of complexity in the negotiation process. The need to have an agreement on common elements to be reported and do it in a consistent and timely manner creates what can be called the inter-linkage dilemma.

4. The Inter-Linkages Dilemma in the Context of Article 6

There are a number of ways to look at inter-linkages solutions. One way would be for "what" is needed to do the accounting to be reported, to be decided under Article 4, as this is where the accounting is being done. This is where the knowledge on the information needed resides.

---

[10]   A complete analysis of the potential inter-linkages between reporting and review requirements and other provisions of the Paris Agreement is in Y. Dagnet et al. 2017. *Mapping the Linkages Between the Transparency Framework and Other Provisions of the Paris Agreement*. World Resources Institute. May. http://www.wri.org/publication/pact-linkages-transparency-framework.

Article 6 negotiators would know what information to provide to fulfill Article 4 requirements, while the transparency negotiators would ensure that the information is included in the required reporting.

It could be argued that the contents of the report is a decision mainly to be taken under Article 6, while how and when to report are decisions to be taken, to some extent, under APA transparency work. The TER should consider how the information is presented and the APA agenda on transparency should also discuss and decide how it should be part of the FMCP.

In this regard, the current list of possible elements listed in the informal note of SBSTA Article 6 could be merged with the list of possible elements listed in the informal note of the APA agenda on transparency, creating agenda items in the next SBSTA meeting.

Once Parties have agreed on what to report under the SBSTA, the APA can decide how these elements should be reported under the biennial transparent report of the Transparency Framework.

In terms of when reporting will be done, the Decisions Adopted by the Conference of the Parties (Decision 1/CP21) has clearly indicated that "all Parties, except for the least developed country Parties and small island developing States, shall submit the information referred to in Article 13, paragraphs 7, 8, 9 and 10, of the Agreement, as appropriate, no less frequently than on a biennial basis, and that the least developed country Parties and small island developing States may submit this information at their discretion."[11] This implies that Parties will report information that tracks progress, including information related to the use of Cooperative Approach and the mechanism on a biennial basis.

This does not preclude the use of national and international registry systems where issuances, transfers, acquisitions, and use of ITMOs and/or greenhouse gas emissions reductions from the mechanism could be continuously reported (i.e., through the use of an international transactional log). Supplementary summary information from these registries could be added to the biennial transparency report. The use of national and international registries is part of the discussions of the guidance for Cooperative Approaches and rules, modalities, and procedures for the mechanism, both under SBSTA.

The information to be reported may vary between Parties, depending on what role each Party has in the Cooperative Approach:

- **Acquiring party.** An acquiring party is participating in a Cooperative Approach, who receives by way of transferring in of an ITMO from another participating party, and who may or may not also be the using party.
- **Using party.** A using party that is participating in a Cooperative Approach who has received the ITMO, accounted for the receipt in accordance with Article 6.2 accounting guidance, and applied it toward its NDC.
- **Issuing party.** An issuing party is participating in a Cooperative Approach, in whose jurisdiction the mitigation action or avoidance of greenhouse gas has occurred.

---

[11] UNFCCC. 2016. *Decisions Adopted by the Conference of the Parties.* Paragraph 91.

- **Transferring party.** A transferring party that is participating in a Cooperative Approach and transfers out an ITMO to an Acquiring Party, for potential use toward its NDC. For the avoidance of doubt with respect to the very first international transfer of an ITMO, the Issuing Party is also the first Transferring Party.

The MPG of the Transparency Framework could indicate, if necessary, the details expected on the tabular information, textual description, and annexes for each type of Party.

In terms of the TER, the information reported on the use of Cooperative Approach will be assessed by the expert teams against the requirements of the "Paris Rulebook," particularly the requirements of the "guidance on accounting under Article 4, paragraph 13," "guidance on cooperative approach," and the "MPG of the Transparency Framework."

For the FMCP, the information reported on the use of Cooperative Approach will be presented and discussed in the context of "implementation and achievement of its nationally determined contribution." Since the Cooperative Approach implies involving two or more participating Parties, the FMCP will have to take into consideration the eventual need to directly include the other Parties involved in the discussions.

To ensure that all provisions and consequential requirements from the Paris Agreement are presented in a consistent and coherent manner in the "Paris Rulebook," it is necessary that the different agenda items under negotiation in different bodies take into consideration all the existent inter-linkages, and allocate clear responsibilities between them and work in an expeditious manner to comply with the 2018 deadline. Article 4 paragraph 13 ("accounting for"); Article 6, paragraph 2 ("Cooperative Approach") and paragraph 4 ("Mechanism"); and Article 13 ("Transparency Framework") illustrate the inter-linkage dilemma.

Key Issues and the Way Forward

The Paris Agreement, which entered into force in November 2016, signifies that Parties are committed to tackling climate change, in a deeper, but very different way from that under the Kyoto Protocol. The Paris Agreement requires that all countries contribute through their respective nationally determined contributions (NDCs), with the expectation that transparency and a global stocktake will encourage an increasing level of ambition from all.

To achieve this, Parties will take action on their own and/or seek international cooperation to achieve their national ambitions to reduce greenhouse gas emissions. Article 6 of the Paris Agreement provides the framework for market and non-market cooperation, including the ability to create international carbon markets, should Parties wish to do so.

The key is that Article 6 provides for the framework of international transfers of mitigation outcomes to be counted toward NDCs. At the same time, it provides for the development of a framework for the most prevalent type of cooperation under the United Nations Framework Convention on Climate Change (UNFCCC), non-market cooperation.

The Paris Agreement entered into force earlier than predicted, and now the work on the preparation of a rulebook is progressing. Article 6 negotiations are to be finalized in December 2018 at the 24th Session of the Conference of the Parties (COP 24) in Poland. This technical publication explores Article 6 of the Paris Agreement to explain the issue and the current status of negotiations.

It is important to remember that Article 6 has a number of components and provide options for Parties to cooperate. The different parts of Article 6 can be seen as being differentiated by the function they provide, and the governance of the cooperation.

Article 6 can be divided into four parts:

- Article 6.1 covers the general concept that Parties may choose, on a voluntary basis, to cooperate in the implementation of their NDCs.
- Articles 6.2 and 6.3 covers the concept that when Parties are involved in the specific case of Cooperative Approaches that involve mitigation outcomes being transferred internationally, they need to observe Conference of the Parties serving as the meeting of the Parties to the Paris Agreement (CMA) guidance on accounting. In short, it creates a framework on how to account for transfers between Parties. It is important to note that the mitigation outcomes seem to be able to emanate from a variety of mitigation approaches (mechanism, procedure, or protocol), without any reference to the fact

that the mechanism, procedure, or protocol needs to operate under the authority of the Conference of the Parties (COP). The main actors are Parties.

- Articles 6.4–6.7 refer to the establishment of a mechanism to produce emissions reduction and support sustainable development, and which operates under the authority of the CMA.
- Article 6.8 establishes a framework for non-market approaches (NMAs). It is unclear yet what may emerge under this Article. While operationalizing the Paris Agreement, Parties will negotiate the details of all these paragraphs.

The Paris Agreement text has many "constructive ambiguities" that were needed to reach an agreement in Paris, which now need to be addressed and decisions need to be made by the Parties on how to interpret and resolve such ambiguities. Such decisions would benefit from some basic elements, which among others include the bottom–up ethos of the Paris Agreement, importance of transparency, the unitary nature of Article 6 and the unitary nature of the Paris Agreement.

This publication examines some of the fundamental issues in Article 6, and brings up some of the questions that need to be answered to complete the Article 6 rulebook in Katowice.

A first issue is the scope of Article 6.2, which may be seen to be the type of activities, mitigation actions, and transfers covered as well as the degree to which Parties will use Article 6.2.

The scope of Article 6.2 is an important issue because it may impact on the ability of Parties to cooperate in any particular manner and ultimately limit the bottom–up ethos of the Agreement. At first glance, the scope of Article 6.2 seems broad, as there is no explicit qualifier restricting its use to mechanisms under the authority of the Conference of the Parties serving as the meeting of the Parties to the Paris Agreement, but limitations do exist and can be classified into two categories: explicit and implicit.

Explicit limitations include provisions in the text of Article 6.2, but the extent to which they are limiting scope depends on how these are operationalized. Implicit limitations are seen as emerging from the text and can be grouped into three categories: what can be transferred, who can transfer, and the characteristics of the internationally transferred mitigation outcomes (ITMO).

Article 6.2 has three "shall provisions" which have not been well elaborated, in terms of definition, governance, and implementation. One of these states that Parties shall ensure "Environmental Integrity". There is still no generally accepted definition of what environmental integrity means in the context of Article 6.2, and Parties have raised a number of requirements on how to ensure it, which can diverge substantially.

There clearly exists considerable ambiguity on how environmental integrity could be operationalized for which three key issues are discussed:

- How can environmental integrity be defined?
- How should environmental integrity be operationalized?
- What is the governance that needs to be put in place?

Article 6.4 of the Paris Agreement provides the "centralized governance option" for the generation and international transfers of mitigation outcomes under Article 6. One view is that it was meant to provide an option with different governance than Article 6.2.

It establishes a mechanism to be "supervised by a body designated by the Conference of the Parties" and creates a centralized window for Parties to deliver mitigation outcomes that can be used toward their NDC or transferred to another party.

Different limitations can also be imagined, and deciding on them will inevitably limit the scope of Article 6.4. This publication makes an effort to address a number of these explicit (e.g., additionality and overall mitigation) and implicit (e.g., eligibility criteria and the relationship between Articles 6.2 and 6.4) limitations and discuss what implications they might have on the scope of Article 6.4.

One critical issue that is of the articulation between Article 6.4 and Article 6.2, or simply put, do mitigation outcomes issued under the Article 6.4 mechanism become ITMOs and are governed under the rules of Article 6.2, or are these on separate tracks, and Article 6.2 and 6.4 mitigation outcomes will not be fungible? These decisions will have strong reverberations, including in the context of double counting.

This brings us to the issue of corresponding adjustments, which is to some degree the heart of the debate for Article 6.2.

Article 6.2 includes another "shall' provision and states that Parties shall apply robust accounting to ensure that double counting is avoided. There remains a lack of clarity associated with the term corresponding adjustments and a number of issues related to its application and understanding.

Decision 1/CP.21, accompanying the Paris Agreement, defines a work program to operationalize the accounting provision in Article 6.2, which states that "guidance should ensure that double counting is avoided on the basis of a corresponding adjustment by Parties ...".

The first issue that needs to be clarified is the difference between accounting and corresponding adjustments. They are two different issues, and should not be mixed-up. A third issue, which is very similar, is that of counting.

Corresponding adjustments will need to be made to ensure that there is no double counting, as well as providing the quantitative position of each Party (surplus or deficit) as a result of transfers under Article 6.2. There are issues that separate it from accounting, which is what needs to be counted, and how to count it toward achieving NDC targets. This issue demands decisions on:

- What transfers can be counted toward the NDC (e.g., certified emission reductions [CERs], Article 6.4 reductions, emission reduction units [ERUs], ITMOs);
- How the transfers that each Party undertakes are counted toward its NDC. This may depend on the timing of these transfers, and the type of the NDC that the Party has formulated.

A second issue is what gets adjusted when applying a corresponding adjustment. Four possible approaches have been examined: target-based, emission-based, buffer registry-based, and emission reduction-based approaches. Regardless of which method or approach to the adjustment is chosen by the Parties, there remains a question as to when the corresponding adjustment will be applied. How corresponding adjustments will be applied in the context of mitigation outcomes produced from inside or outside the scope of the NDCs still needs discussion and resolution among Parties.

Many Parties have decided to use single-year targets in their NDCs. This could be challenging for corresponding adjustments as there is uncertainty over the emissions pathway in non-target years. There are several options available to deal with this issue.

Even if corresponding adjustments are referenced in relation to Article 6.2 only, as the discussion around the scope of Article 6.2 and its relationship with Article 6.4 has indicated, corresponding adjustments will also need to be considered in the case of Article 6.4, both when the initial mitigation outcome is created, as well as at further transfers.

The third part of Article 6 concerns the establishment of a framework for NMAs. It remains unclear what will be covered under this framework, but some focus is starting to emerge. Contrary to Articles 6.2 and 6.4, a work program has to be decided instead of guidance notes, rules, modalities and procedures.

There are two major possibilities on the role of this framework:

- It should provide for sharing experience and best practices.
- It should provide for enhanced support to developing countries through finance and capacity-building for the implementation of NMAs.

This publication seeks to explore the possible scope of what could constitute a NMA, what the scope of the work program could entail and what governance could be envisaged following different expectations on what the role of the framework will be.

For the operationalization of the Paris Agreement, decisions will have to be taken on several provisions, established by different articles. Some of these provisions have inter-linkages, i.e., decisions taken in relation to one article may affect decisions to be taken in relation to another article and vice versa.

Of particular interest for Article 6 will be the decision on the reporting and reviewing requirements of information submitted under Article 13 of the Paris Agreement, the Transparency Framework, as they include information related to the use of Articles 6.2 and 6.4. This publication explores the relevant inter-linkages between these different negotiation items, and the dilemma associated with their inter-linkages in the context of Article 6.

Way Forward

Discussions on Article 6 are intensifying as the negotiation process is approaching a critical step: the adoption of the Paris Agreement rulebook at COP 24 in Katowice in December 2018.

The upcoming meeting in Bonn, which takes place under the Subsidiary Body for Scientific and Technical Advice (SBSTA) in early May 2018, is one of the few remaining negotiation meetings Parties can use to develop the rulebook. SBSTA is one of the technical committees that prepare draft decisions and elaborations for the COP and is responsible for drafting the guidance, rules, modalities, and procedures for Article 6.

Finalizing the rulebook by COP 24 is challenging given the amount of work remaining. For sure, negotiators will continue to elaborate all rules, guidance, modalities, procedures, and work programs also after COP 24, but there is hope that key elements will be defined by end of 2018.

Once we pass SBSTA 48, the additional negotiating sessions that are expected in September, and then COP24 in Katowice, will give the negotiators opportunity to discover what remains to be done. The expectation should be that the decisions that will make Article 6.2 operational should be in place, and that details on what would need to be included in as part of reporting under the transparency framework may need to continue past COP24. That is based on the assumption of relatively decentralized governance for Article 6.2, with no new bodies being created that would necessitate modalities and procedures.

Article 6.4 is likely to require significant new work, which will be undertaken under the new Supervisory Body, which we expect to be installed at COP 24. This new body may have to come back with draft modalities and procedures for CMA approval at COP 25. It may also be tasked to propose to the CMA at COP 25 those elements (baselines, DOE accreditation, etc.) which it intends to retain intact, or in a modified form from the Clean Development Mechanism and Joint Implementation.

For market participants, the post COP 24 period will also be busy as pilots will undoubtedly be undertaken to test how Article 6.2 transactions are undertaken and to assess what capacity and infrastructure needs to put in place. These are all new elements, especially for developing countries, but not only. ITMO standards will need to be developed between cooperating Parties in such a way that we do not end up in a race to the bottom from an environmental integrity point of view. Finally, supply and demand will have to be developed, with new funds for Article 6.4 likely to emerge, and with new financial instruments to developed demands also in need of work.

All in all, the hard, practical work is just about to begin.

Framework Convention on
Climate Change

SBSTA48.Informal.2

Subsidiary Body for Scientific and Technological Advice
Forty-eighth session
Bonn, 30 April to 10 May 2018

16 March 2018

Informal document containing the draft elements of guidance on cooperative approaches referred to in Article 6, paragraph 2, of the Paris Agreement

Informal document by the Chair

Contents

Introduction

A.   Mandate

1.   Article 6, paragraph 2 of the Paris Agreement refers to voluntary cooperative approaches that involve the use of internationally transferred mitigation outcomes towards nationally determined contributions. By decision 1/CP.21, paragraph 36, the Conference of the Parties requested the Subsidiary Body for Scientific and Technological Advice (SBSTA) to develop and recommend guidance referred to in Article 6, paragraph 2, for adoption by the Conference of the Parties serving as the meeting of the Parties to the Paris Agreement (CMA) at its first session.

2.   At SBSTA 47, to facilitate the deliberations at SBSTA 48, the SBSTA requested the SBSTA Chair to prepare an informal document containing the draft elements of guidance on cooperative approaches based on prior submissions by Parties under this agenda sub-item and the third iteration of the informal note prepared by the co-chairs of the relevant agenda item[1] (hereinafter referred to as the third iteration note).

B.   Scope

3.   The annex to this informal document contains the draft elements of guidance prepared by the SBSTA Chair on the basis of the above mandate (hereinafter referred to as the draft elements of guidance).

C.   Approach

4.   The SBSTA Chair has developed the draft elements of guidance based on the third iteration note and previous submissions by the Parties under this agenda sub-item.

5.   The draft elements of guidance have, in relation to the third iteration note, sought to:

(a)   Streamline the structure, including removing duplication, without removing elements;

(b)   Bring the elements of each issue together to facilitate discussions at SBSTA 48;

(c)   Develop the language for the implementation of elements from the third iteration note, without developing full text;

(d)   Clarify options and the potential further elements to be considered.

6.   In the draft elements of guidance, all paragraphs and sub-paragraphs have been numbered sequentially to make it easier for Parties to identify substantive content of the options when using the informal document to facilitate discussions at SBSTA 48.

7.   Generally, throughout the draft elements of guidance, curly brackets containing italicized text ("{*curly brackets containing italicized text*}") are used to provide information about the relevant element.

8.   Where the draft elements of guidance contain options, these are labelled as "**Option A**", "**Option B**", etc. To assist navigation of the text, options are followed by a brief indicative narrative, in curly brackets and in bolded, italicised text ("{***narrative of the option***}"). Where, within a section of the draft elements of guidance, the end of the last option in a group of options is followed by other elements that are not part of those options, the phrase "{*end of Option X*}" is inserted for clarity. No options extend beyond a section into the next section.

9.   Where an element/option has several potential sub-elements, the note "{*potential list below*}" is included just before the list begins, in order to show Parties that they need to consider each sub-element independently, and not as a group of sub-elements. The note "{*further potential list below*}"

---

[1]   http://unfccc.int/cooperation_support/cooperative_implementation/items/9644.php and
http://unfccc.int/documentation/documents/advanced_search/items/6911.php?priref=600009936.

3

is used in a similar manner for sub-sub-elements. That note is not used where the sub-elements are a suite and are needed together.

10. Where it appears that further development of a potential element/option would be required for implementation, the following note is made: "{*further development may be required for implementation*}", and in some cases, further possible action or examples are identified in order to help Parties identify what further development might include.

11. Where, within a sentence, there are alternatives or choices that may be selected, a forward slash ("/") has been used to indicate those alternatives in the sentence, so that the sentence remains readable as a whole. However, where there is "and/or", this means "and" as well as "or".

12. Where there is provision for a certain number of events to be organised, members to be appointed, etc. the draft elements of guidance use "*X*", "*Y*", "*Z*" etc. to indicate choices that would need to be taken.

13. The selection of certain options may have implications on other options in other sections of the draft elements of guidance. In order to keep the document manageable, not all consequential implications for other parts of the draft elements of guidance are indicated. In certain cases, some options are incompatible with some other options in other sections and, where this is particularly acute, the draft elements of guidance identify that in curly brackets.

14. Furthermore, the draft elements of guidance cannot assess all the possible ways in which options which are found in different parts of the text might be combined. It should be noted, however, that the structure and coherence of the overall text will have particularly important consequences for meeting the requirement in Article 6, paragraph 2 of the Paris Agreement to ensure environmental integrity.

15. There is a technical interconnection between these draft elements of guidance and the draft elements of the rules, modalities and procedures for the mechanism established by Article 6, paragraph 4, of the Paris Agreement, as set out in informal document SBSTA48.Informal.3.

16. The draft elements of guidance also use the following phrases solely for the purposes of keeping the draft elements of guidance short and readable (and without prejudice to their definition at a later stage by the SBSTA):

(a) "**ITMO**" is the abbreviation for "internationally transferred mitigation outcome". In certain places, it may be more accurate to refer to a "mitigation outcome" (i.e. a mitigation outcome that has not yet been internationally transferred) or to a "unit", but unless it is essential to understand the element, the term ITMO has been used;

(b) Where there is reference to "**sector/greenhouse gases**" covered by the NDC of a Party, this focuses on the mitigation part of the nationally determined contribution (NDC), while recognizing that the NDC may contain other parts;

(c) "**creation**" of ITMOs means creation including, where relevant, issuance of ITMOs or units;

(d) "**transfer**" means international transfer everywhere it is used (except in the term ITMO) and **first transfer** means the first time ITMOs are transferred internationally. Thus, transfers within a Party are not covered directly in the draft elements of guidance;

(e) "**use, uses**" is in the context of use towards the achievement of the NDC. The use of an ITMO towards achievement of a NDC could be effected through retirement or cancellation of ITMOs or by other means, but at this stage the draft elements of guidance have not elaborated that aspect;

(f) "**NDC implementation period**" is used to mean the period from the start to the end of the NDC;

(g) "**single year**" also means final or target year, when used to refer to NDCs.

D. Possible Actions by the Subsidiary Body for Scientific and Technological Advice

17. The SBSTA may wish to consider this informal document, and refine and elaborate the draft elements of guidance contained herein.

SBSTA.48.Informal.2

Annex

Draft elements of guidance on cooperative approaches

I.   Preamble {*potential list below*}

Pp1   *Recalling* Article 2 of the Paris Agreement.

Pp2   *Recalling* Article 2 of the Paris Agreement and decision 1/CP.21, paragraph 1.

Pp3   *Recalling* Article 2 of the Paris Agreement and its paragraph 1.

II.   Principles

Option A {*list of principles*} {*potential list below*}

1.   Parties engaging in cooperative approaches under Article 6, paragraph 2, of the Paris Agreement[1] (hereinafter referred to as cooperative approaches) that involve the use of internationally transferred mitigation outcomes (ITMOs) towards achievement of nationally determined contributions (NDCs) to be guided by the following principles {*further potential list below*}:

(a)   In accordance with Article 6, paragraph 1, participation in cooperative approaches is voluntary;

(b)   Pursuant to Article 6, paragraph 1, cooperative approaches allow Parties to maintain current ambition in their NDC and allow for higher mitigation and adaptation ambition;

(c)   In accordance with Article 6, paragraph 2, cooperative approaches to promote sustainable development;

(d)   In accordance with Article 6, paragraph 2, cooperative approaches to ensure environmental integrity. Ensuring environmental integrity includes ensuring that such cooperative approaches do not lead to an overall increase in global greenhouse gas emissions;

(e)   In accordance with Article 6, paragraph 2, Parties to ensure transparency, including in governance;

(f)   In accordance with Article 6, paragraph 2, Parties to apply robust accounting and ensure the avoidance of double counting;

(g)   Pursuant to Article 4, paragraph 3, cooperative approaches to be consistent with the participating Parties' NDC and be designed and implemented in a manner that supports progression beyond the participating Parties' current NDC;

(h)   The nature of its NDC not to exclude any Party from participating in cooperative approaches;

(i)   Cooperative approaches to "be bottom up" and to maintain national prerogatives by ensuring that such cooperative approaches are led by participating Parties;

(j)   Cooperative approaches to prioritize implementation of the participating Parties' NDC, and avoid extraneous influences;

(k)   Cooperative approaches to take into consideration Article 4, paragraphs 7 and 15;

(l)   Participating Parties to avoid unilateral measures and discriminatory practices in such cooperative approaches;

(m)   Cooperative approaches to be implemented through a multilateral rules-based system.

2.   The Conference of the Parties serving as the meeting of the Parties to the Paris Agreement (CMA) to ensure consistency between this guidance and the rules, modalities and procedures for the

---

[1] References to "Article" are to articles of the Paris Agreement, unless otherwise specified.

5

mechanism established by Article 6, paragraph 4, in relation to the use of emission reductions under that mechanism towards achievement of NDCs.

Option B {*no list of principles*}

{*no text required*}

III. Scope

3.   This guidance to apply to {*potential list below*}:

(a)   Parties engaging in cooperative approaches on a voluntary basis;

(b)   Creation, transfer, acquisition, use of ITMOs towards achievement of an NDC;

(c)   The following greenhouse gases {*further development may be required for implementation, including, for example, reference to IPCC/NDCs of participating Parties*};

(d)   How Parties make a corresponding adjustment for both anthropogenic emissions by sources and removals by sinks covered by their NDC and the timing of that corresponding adjustment;

(e)   Cooperative approaches under Article 6, paragraph 2, and mitigation activities under the mechanism established by Article 6, paragraph 4;

(f)   The creation of ITMOs under Article 6, paragraph 2, other than emission reductions certified and issued pursuant to the rules, modalities and procedures for the mechanism established by Article 6, paragraph 4.

Option A {*special circumstances of LDCs and SIDs*}

4.   In relation to least developed countries and small island developing States, the special circumstances of least developed countries and small island developing States as set out in Article 4, paragraph 6, to be recognized where this guidance relates to NDCs {*further development may be required for implementation*}.

Option B {*no special circumstances*}

{*no text required*}

IV. Purpose

5.   This guidance to {*potential list below*}:

(a)   Ensure consistency of cooperative approaches with Article 2;

(b)   Ensure consistency of cooperative approaches with Article 6, paragraph 1.

V. Definitions

6.   For the purposes of this guidance for cooperative approaches under Article 6, paragraph 2, the definitions contained in Article 1 and the provisions of Article 17 to apply. Furthermore {*potential list below*}:

(a)   An "**acquiring Party**" is a Party to the Paris Agreement to which an ITMO is transferred;

(b)   A "**corresponding adjustment**" is an adjustment that is consistent with this guidance and made by a Party/the Parties participating in a cooperative approach;

(c)   A "**creating Party**" is a Party to the Paris Agreement that creates and/or issues an ITMO that may be used towards achievement of an NDC and is the Party that may make a first international transfer (first transfer) of an ITMO;

(d)   "**Double counting**", as per Article 6, paragraph 2, means double claiming, double issuance, double registration or double use:

(i)   "**Double claiming**" is any of the following:

    a.   The use by more than one Party of an ITMO/mitigation outcome towards achievement of its NDC;

    b.   The use by one Party of an ITMO towards achievement of its NDC and the use by the same, or another, Party of the same ITMO/mitigation outcome for a purpose other than towards achievement of its NDC;

(ii)   "**Double issuance**" is the issuance, by a Party, in the same or different metrics of two or more ITMOs for the same mitigation outcome;

(iii)   "**Double registration**" means that the same activity and/or ITMO/mitigation outcome is registered or equivalent under two or more cooperative approaches/non-UNFCCC or other programmes/the mechanism established in Article 6, paragraph 4;

(iv)   "**Double use**" is any of the following:

    a.   The use by one Party of an ITMO towards achievement of its NDC more than once;

    b.   The use by one Party of an ITMO towards achievement of its NDC and the use by the same or another Party of that ITMO for a purpose other than towards achievement of its NDC;

(e)   "**Environmental integrity**" in Article 6, paragraph 2, includes the following {*potential list below*}:

(i)   That cooperative approaches do not lead to an overall increase in global greenhouse gas emissions;

(ii)   That participating Parties' first transfer and use of ITMOs towards achievement of an NDC or transfer and acquisition of ITMOs does not lead to an overall increase in global greenhouse gas emissions {*linked to section X (Corresponding adjustment)*};

(iii)   That ITMOs created, transferred, acquired, or used towards achievement of NDCs are real, permanent, additional and verifiable.

(f)   An "**internationally transferred mitigation outcome**" and "**ITMO**" have the meaning given to it in section VI (Internationally transferred mitigation outcomes);

(g)   "**Overall mitigation in global emissions**" takes place when the mitigation resulting from a cooperative approach is delivered at a level that goes beyond what would be achieved through the delivery of NDCs of participating Parties in aggregate;

(h)   "**Registry**" means an electronic system that meets the requirements of section XIII.B (Registry) including a registry maintained by the secretariat;

(i)   A "**transferring Party**" is a Party to the Paris Agreement from which an ITMO is transferred;

(j)   A "**using Party**" is a Party to the Paris Agreement that uses ITMOs towards achievement of its NDC, including through retirement or cancellation.

    {*further definitions may be required for implementation*}

VI.   Internationally transferred mitigation outcomes

A.   Internationally transferred mitigation outcomes that may be used towards achievement of a nationally determined contribution

7.   An ITMO to be consistent with the guidance in this section VI.

1.   Responsibility

8.   The responsibility to elaborate what may be an ITMO that may be used towards achievement of an NDC to be with:

SBSTA48.Informal.2

Option A {*the CMA*}

(a)   the CMA;

Option B {*the 6.2 body*}

(b)   the 6.2 body;

Option C {*participating Parties*}

(c)   participating Parties implementing a cooperative approach.

2.   **Measurement**

Option A {*guidance on measurement*}

9.   An ITMO to be {*potential list below*}:

(a)   Equal to one metric tonne of carbon dioxide equivalent (CO_2e);

(b)   Measured in a metric other than tonnes of CO_2e;

10.   An ITMO to be calculated {*potential list below*}:

(a)   In accordance with the methodologies and common metrics assessed by the IPCC and adopted by the COP/CMA;

(b)   Using global warming potentials assessed/recommended by the IPCC and adopted by the COP/CMA.

Option B {*no guidance on measurement*}

{*no text required*}

3.   **Form**

Option A {*guidance on form*}

11.   An ITMO to be {*potential list below*}:

(a)   A unit;

(b)   A net flow between participating Parties in a given period.

Option B {*no guidance on form*}

{*no text required*}

4.   **Scope**

Option A {*guidance on scope*}

12.   An ITMO may be created for {*potential list below*}:

(a)   Emission reductions;

(b)   Emission removals;

(c)   Emissions avoided;

(d)   The full spectrum of mitigation outcomes, including mitigation co-benefits of adaptation actions and/or economic diversification plans;

(e)   Net absolute national reductions.

Option B {*no guidance on scope*}

{*no text required*}

B.   Characteristics of an internationally transferred mitigation outcome

13.   ITMOs to have the following characteristics {*potential list below*}:

(a)   Be real, permanent, additional and verifiable;

(b)   If a unit, have a unique serial number comprising the following elements {*further development may be required for implementation, for example Party of origin code*};

(c)   To be consistently identified and defined by the participating Parties.

C.   Other internationally transferred mitigation outcomes

14.   The following are also ITMOs {*potential list below*}:

(a)   Those emission reductions issued and subject to a corresponding adjustment under this guidance as per the rules, modalities and procedures for the mechanism established by Article 6, paragraph 4 {*further development may be required for implementation*};

(b)   Certified emission reductions issued under Article 12 of the Kyoto Protocol that are used towards achievement of an NDC {*further development may be required for implementation*};

(c)   Emission reduction units determined under Article 6 of the Kyoto Protocol that are used towards achievement of an NDC {*further development may be required for implementation*}.

VII.   Governance

A.   Role of the Conference of the Parties serving as the meeting of the Parties to the Paris Agreement

Option A {*CMA functions, including issuance process*}

15.   The CMA to {*potential list below*}:

(a)   Approve creation of/issue ITMOs, in accordance with this guidance;

(b)   Periodically review the participation of non-Party actors to provide further guidance, as necessary.

Option B {*no CMA functions*}

{*no text required*} {*end of Option B*}

16.   The CMA to review this guidance periodically/by no later than {*X date*}, on the basis of recommendations from {*further development may be required for implementation*}.

B.   Oversight arrangements

Option A {*Article 6.2 body*}

17.   A cooperative approaches body (hereinafter referred to as the "6.2 body") to ensure consistency with this guidance {*further development may be required for implementation*} and to {*potential list below*}:

(a)   Review the information submitted by a Party in accordance with section IX.B (Ex-ante review);

(b)   Review the information submitted by a Party in accordance with section XI.B (Periodic and ex-post review);

(c)   Approve creation of/issue ITMOs from cooperative approaches consistent with this guidance {*further development may be required for implementation*};

(d)   Oversee a third-party review of the environmental integrity of ITMOs at creation {*further development may be required for implementation*}.

Option B {*Article 13 review or other expert review to review for consistency with this guidance*}

18. Each participating Party to ensure its participation in cooperative approaches and its use of ITMOs towards achievement of its NDC is consistent with this guidance.

19. The expert review to review for consistency with this guidance and to {*potential list below*}:

(a) Review the information submitted by a Party in accordance with section IX.B (Ex-ante review);

(b) Review the information submitted by a Party in accordance with section XI.B (Periodic and ex-post review).

C. Role of the secretariat {*further development may be required for implementation*}

20. Pursuant to Article 17, and consistent with this guidance, the secretariat to {*potential list below*}:

(a) Maintain a centralized accounting database;

(b) Maintain a multilateral registry for Parties that do not wish to have their own registry;

(c) Administer an international transaction log to record, validate and verify transactions, including creation and first transfers, transfers, acquisition, and use towards achievement of an NDC of ITMOs;

(d) Compile and cross-reference information and check information submitted on corresponding adjustments;

(e) Make available information to the public on {*further development may be required for implementation*}.

21. The secretariat to report {*further development may be required for implementation*} {*potential list below*}:

(a) Annually to the CMA on the share of proceeds collected pursuant to section XVI (Share of proceeds);

(b) Annually to the CMA on the overall mitigation in global emissions achieved pursuant to section XV.A (Overall mitigation in global emissions);

(c) On progress made by Parties in implementing and achieving NDCs, based on the information contained in the centralized accounting database.

D. Role of other actors {*further development may be required for implementation*}

22. Non-Party actors may, where applicable subject to authorization by a participating Party: {*potential list below*}:

(a) Participate in cooperative approaches;

(b) Transfer and acquire ITMOs;

(c) Use ITMOs for purposes other than towards achievement of an NDC.

VIII. Participation requirements

23. A Party may participate on a voluntary basis in cooperative approaches if the Party meets the following requirements {*potential list below*}:

(a) It is a Party to the Paris Agreement;

(b) It has prepared, communicated and is currently maintaining an NDC in accordance with Article 4, paragraph 2;

(c) It has authorized the use of ITMOs pursuant to Article 6, paragraph 3 and has made that authorization public {*further development may be required for implementation*};

(d) It has designated a national authority/focal point and has communicated that designation to the secretariat;

(e) It has a registry or access to a registry that meets the requirements of section XIV.A (Registry) below;

(f) It has a system or access to a system for recording the origin, creation, transfer, acquisition and use towards achievement of its NDC of ITMOs;

(g) It has provided the most recently required inventory report in accordance with the modalities, procedures and guidelines relating to Article 13, paragraph 7, including a consistent time series of inventory emissions submitted no less than annually/biennially;

(h) It has formulated and communicated an economy-wide long-term low-emission development strategy pursuant to Article 4, paragraph 19;

(i) In relation to quantification of its current NDC, it has done the following for the purposes of participating in cooperative approaches {*further potential list below*}:

    (i) Quantified the mitigation into an amount of tonnes of CO_2e;

    (ii) Identified the sectors and greenhouse gases covered by its NDC;

    (iii) Identified the time period for its NDC (e.g. multi-year or single year);

    (iv) Calculated an absolute-emissions, multi-year, economy-wide target;

    (v) Identified an indicative emissions trajectory consistent with its long-term low greenhouse gas emission development strategy pursuant to Article 4, paragraph 19;

(j) In relation to each cooperative approach {*further potential list below*}:

    (i) It has a process to set a baseline;

    (ii) It has requirements to mitigate leakage risk;

    (iii) It has systems to ensure permanence, including to address reversals;

(k) In relation to ITMOs {*further potential list below*}:

    (i) It has a process to verify ITMOs created and first transferred;

    (ii) It has a process to ensure that ITMOs created and first transferred and/or used do not result in environmental harm {*further development may be required for implementation*};

    (iii) It has a process to ensure that ITMOs created and first transferred and/or used do not adversely affect human rights {*further development may be required for implementation*};

IX.   Ex-ante Party reporting and review

A.   Ex-ante reporting

Option A {*ex-ante reporting contains information required in Participation requirements*}

24.   Each Party intending to participate in cooperative approaches to provide, prior to its participation in cooperative approaches, the information required in section VIII (Participation requirements) to demonstrate that it meets the participation requirements {*further development may be required for implementation*}.

Option B {*ex-ante reporting contains all the following steps*}

25.   Each Party intending to participate in cooperative approaches to provide the following information in the following steps:

(a) Quantification of allowable emissions through calculating how many tonnes of CO_2e could be emitted while achieving its NDC;

(b) Multiplied by the number of years in the NDC, converted into a number of units, each corresponding to one tonne of CO_2e;

(c) Where that number exceeds the average annual emissions for the years preceding the NDC, as per the last three national inventories, the difference, multiplied by the number of years in the NDC to be reserved for domestic use only;

(d) The resulting figure represents the quantified NDC.

B. Ex-ante review

Option A {*ex-ante review by the 6.2 body*} {*potential list below*}

26. Following submission by a Party of the information contained in section IX.A above, the 6.2 body to review the information for consistency with the participation requirements.

27. A Party may participate where the ex-ante review determines that it meets the participation requirements {*further development may be required for implementation*}.

Option B {*ex ante review by expert review*} {*potential list below*}

28. Following submission by a Party of the information contained in section IX.A above, the expert review to review the information for consistency with this guidance.

29. A Party may participate where the ex-ante review determines that it meets the participation requirements {*further development may be required for implementation*}.

30. Where relevant, a Party to issue units up to the allowable emissions, following the technical expert review {*relates to budget-based below and Option B in section IX. A (Ex-ante reporting)*}.

Option C {*no ex-ante review*}

{*No text required*}

X. Corresponding adjustment

A. Article 6, paragraph 2, corresponding adjustment

1. General

Option A {*all Parties use the same basis for corresponding adjustment*}

31. A Party to apply the basis for corresponding adjustment set out in section X.2 below consistently throughout the NDC implementation period {*further development may be required for implementation*}.

Option B {*a Party chooses which basis for corresponding adjustment and applies it consistently*}

32. A Party to select one of the bases for corresponding adjustment set out in section X.2 below and apply it consistently throughout the NDC implementation period {*further development may be required for implementation*}.

2. Basis for Article 6, paragraph 2, corresponding adjustment

Option A {*budget-based*} {*see Option B in section IX.A (Ex ante reporting) and section XII.A (Specific guidance for budget-based)*}

33. Budget-based, where a Party applies the corresponding adjustment to a quantified budget of allowable emissions based on its quantified NDC.

Option B {*emissions-based*}

34. Emissions-based, where a Party applies the corresponding adjustment to relevant emissions derived from greenhouse gas emissions totals in its national inventory, with a resulting balance (e.g. accounting balance).

12

Option C {*buffer registry based*}

35.   A buffer registry where a Party applies the corresponding adjustment for each transfer and acquisition from a starting point of a zero balance, with a resulting balance that reflects net transfers and acquisitions.

Option D {*emission reductions based*}

36.   Emission reductions based, where the Party calculates the total quantity of emission reductions required in order for it to achieve its NDC and applies a corresponding adjustment to that total {*further development required for implementation*}.

B.   Application of corresponding adjustment

Option A {*Parties make a corresponding adjustment for first transfer and for use towards achievement of NDC*}

Option A1 {*budget-based*}

37.   Party to effect a subtraction for all ITMOs created and transferred for the first time.

38.   Party to effect an addition for all ITMOs used towards achievement of its NDC.

Option A2 {*emissions-based*}

39.   Party to effect an addition for all ITMOs created and transferred for the first time.

40.   Party to effect a subtraction for all ITMOs used towards achievement of its NDC.

Option A3 {*buffer registry based*}

{*not applicable to buffer registry based, no text required*}

Option A4 {*emission reductions based*}

41.   Party to effect an addition for all ITMOs created and transferred for the first time.

42.   Party to effect a subtraction for all ITMOs used towards achievement of its NDC.

Option B {*Parties make a corresponding adjustment for transfers and acquisitions*}

Option B1 {*budget-based*}

43.   Party to effect a subtraction for all ITMOs transferred.

44.   Party to effect an addition for all ITMOs acquired.

Option B2 {*emissions-based*}

45.   Party to effect an addition for all ITMOs transferred.

46.   Party to effect a subtraction for all ITMOs acquired.

Option B3 {*buffer registry-based*}

47.   Party to effect an addition for all ITMOs transferred.

48.   Party to effect a subtraction for all ITMOs acquired.

Option B4 {*emission reductions based*}

49.   Party to effect an addition for all ITMOs transferred.

50.   Party to effect a subtraction for all ITMOs acquired.

C.   Frequency of the corresponding adjustment {*further development may be required for implementation*}

Option A {*real-time*}

51.   Parties to make the corresponding adjustment at the time of each of:

(a)   First transfer and use {*where the corresponding adjustment is for creation, first transfer and use*};

(b)   Transfer and acquisition {*where the corresponding adjustment is for transfer and acquisition*}.

Option B {*periodic, e.g. annually, biennially, matching reporting period*}

52.   Parties to make the corresponding adjustment periodically and/or reflect the corresponding adjustment in the reporting referred to in this guidance.

Option C {*when demonstrating achievement of NDC*}

53.   Parties to make the corresponding adjustment when demonstrating use of ITMOs towards achievement of its NDC.

XI.   Periodic and ex-post Party reporting and review

A.   Periodic and ex-post Party reporting

Option A {*periodic: annually, biennially, matching reporting period*} and

Option B {*when demonstrating achievement of NDC*}

54.   Each participating Party to provide, at the end of the reporting period/NDC implementation period, the following information {*potential list below*}:

(a)   In relation to tracking ITMOs {*further potential list below*}:

    (i)   Total cumulative NDC relevant emissions over the reporting period/NDC implementation period;

    (ii)   Total cumulative ITMOs created and first transferred, transferred and acquired, and used towards achievement of its NDC and over the reporting period/NDC implementation period;

    (iii)   The balance for the reporting period/NDC implementation period;

    (iv)   How it has used ITMOs towards achievement of its NDC;

(b)   In relation to the ITMOs {*potential list below*}:

    (i)   Evidence of authorization pursuant to Article 6, paragraph 3;

    (ii)   The Party origin and the originating cooperative approach of the ITMOs;

    (iii)   The characteristics of the ITMOs (e.g. the metric, sector, vintage);

    (iv)   How it has ensured the ITMOs are real, permanent, additional and verified;

    (v)   How it has ensured the environmental integrity of the ITMOs (including that transfers have not increased global emissions, that use does not erode the using Party's NDC);

    (vi)   How it has ensured that ITMOs used towards achievement of its NDC will not be further transferred, acquired or used (e.g. through cancellation, retirement of such ITMOs);

    (vii)   Provision of information in a standard reporting table/format {*further development may be required for implementation*};

(c)   How the registry in section XIV.A (Registry) meets the requirements of this guidance;

(d)   In relation to cooperative approaches and use of ITMOs towards achievement of the NDC of the Party {*potential list below*}:

    (i)   How it has ensured the environmental integrity of cooperative approaches;

    (ii)   How the cooperative approaches support implementation of its NDC and/or the mitigation of greenhouse gas emissions;

(iii)   How any participation by the Party in the mechanism established under Article 6, paragraph 4, supports implementation of its NDC and/or the mitigation of greenhouse gas emissions;

(iv)   How the cooperative approaches are consistent with its long-term low greenhouse gas emission development strategy pursuant to Article 4, paragraph 19 and foster transition to a low emissions economy;

(v)   How the creation, first transfer and use and/or the transfer and acquisition of ITMOs is consistent with Article 3 in relation to progression over time;

(vi)   How the use of ITMOs promotes sustainable development in the creating Party;

(vii)   How the creation, first transfer and use and/or transfer and acquisition of ITMOs promotes sustainable development within the context of the national prerogatives of that Party and/or within the context of its implementation of the Sustainable Development Goals;

(viii)   How the creation, first transfer and use and/or transfer and acquisition of ITMOs avoided environmental harm;

(ix)   How the creation, first transfer and use and/or transfer and acquisition of ITMOs avoided a violation of human rights;

(x)   Any updates to its methods for accounting for progress pursuant to the modalities, procedures and guidelines relating to Article 13, paragraph 7.

B.   Periodic and ex-post review

Option A {*periodic and/or ex-post review*}

Option A1 {*review by the 6.2 body*} {*potential list below*}

55.   Following submission by a Party of the information under section XI.A (Periodic and ex-post Party reporting), the 6.2 body to review the information for consistency with this guidance, including {*potential list below*}:

(a)   Standards and methodologies used in the cooperative approach;

(b)   Whether the Party has used approved methodologies and baseline approaches for cooperative approaches that are no less rigorous than similar methodologies and baseline approaches approved under the mechanism established by Article 6, paragraph 4;

(c)   Review the information submitted by the Party through comparison and cross-checking of information submitted.

56.   The 6.2 body to oversee the correction of accounting/corresponding adjustment errors identified with regard to ITMOs used towards achievement of its NDC.

57.   Following its review, the 6.2 body to determine whether the Party's participation in cooperative approaches is consistent with this guidance.

Option A2 {*review conducted by technical expert review*} {*potential list below*}

58.   Following submission by a Party of the information under section XI.A (Periodic and ex-post Party reporting), the technical expert review to review the information for consistency with this guidance, including {*further development may be required for implementation*}.

59.   Following its review, the technical expert review to provide assurance {*further development may be required for implementation*}.

Option B {*no review*}

{*No text required*}

XII.   Specific guidance

A.   Budget-based corresponding adjustment

Option A {*specific multilateral rules-based guidance for budget-based*}

60.   Party to calculate the quantified NDC in accordance with section IX.A (Ex-ante reporting) {*requires Option B of that section*}.

61.   Party to issue units in accordance with section XI.B (Ex-ante review) {*requires Option B of that section*}.

62.   Party to make corresponding adjustment in accordance with section X above (Corresponding adjustment).

63.   Party to identify the difference between allowable emissions and average actual reported emissions in the three years preceding the NDC period and any positive difference to be transferred into an NDC time frame reserve and used only for meeting its own NDC.

64.   At end of NDC implementation period, the Party to retire the number of units equal to NDC relevant emissions.

Option B {*no specific guidance*}

{*no text required*}

B.   Sectors/greenhouse gases etc.

1.   General

65.   A creating Party may create and first transfer an ITMO that is achieved in its jurisdiction:

Option A {*only inside NDC*}

(a)   in sectors/greenhouse gases covered by that Party's NDC;

Option B {*sectors inside and outside NDC*}

(b)   in any sector/greenhouse gases, whether or not they are covered by that Party's NDC.

2.   Sectors/greenhouse gases covered by the nationally determined contribution

66.   For ITMOs that are created and first transferred by a Party and achieved in sectors/greenhouse gases covered by that Party's NDC, each participating Party to make a corresponding adjustment in accordance with section X (Corresponding adjustment).

3.   Sectors/greenhouse gases not covered by the nationally determined contribution {*this section is dependent on section XII.A.1 above and applies only for Option B*}

67.   For ITMOs that are created and first transferred by a Party and achieved outside the sectors/greenhouse gases covered by that Party's NDC:

(a)   The using Party to make a corresponding adjustment in accordance with section X (Corresponding adjustment);

(b)   The creating Party to:

Option A {*make a corresponding adjustment*}

(i)   make a corresponding adjustment in accordance with section X (Corresponding adjustment);

Option B {*no corresponding adjustment, reporting only*}

(ii)   report in accordance with this guidance {*further development may be required for implementation*}.

Option C {*no action required*}

{*no text required*}

C.   Single-year nationally determined contributions

68.   A Party that has a single-year NDC to apply the guidance in this section.

Option A {*single-year vintage creation and transfer only*}

Option A1 {*where the corresponding adjustment is for creation, first transfer and use*}

69.   A Party to only create, first transfer and use towards achievement of its NDC ITMOs that were achieved in the same year as its single-year NDC.

Option A2 {*where the corresponding adjustment is for transfer and acquisition*}

70.   A Party to only transfer and acquire ITMOs that were achieved in the same year as its single-year NDC.

Option B {*cumulative corresponding adjustments*}

Option B1{*where the corresponding adjustment is for creation, first transfer and use*}

71.   A Party that creates and first transfers ITMOs to make a corresponding adjustment in the single year for the total amount of ITMOs created and first transferred over the NDC implementation period and a Party that uses ITMOs towards achievement of its NDC to make corresponding adjustment in the single year for the total amount of ITMOs used over the NDC implementation period.

Option B2 {*where the corresponding adjustment is for transfer and acquisition*}

72.   A Party that transfers and acquires ITMOs achieved in the years of its NDC implementation period to make a corresponding adjustment in the single year of its NDC for the total amount of ITMOs transferred/acquired over the entire NDC implementation period.

Option C {*comparison to a trend that would be consistent with NDC achievement*}

Option C1 {*where the corresponding adjustment is for creation, first transfer and use*}

73.   A Party to calculate a trajectory in relation to emissions for the NDC implementation period that is consistent with the achievement of its NDC in the single year and to make a corresponding adjustment for each year of the NDC implementation period equal to the total amount of ITMOs that it creates and first transfers and/or uses towards achievement of its NDC.

Option C2 {*where the corresponding adjustment is for transfer and acquisition*}

74.   A Party to calculate a trajectory in relation to emissions for the NDC implementation period that is consistent with the achievement of its NDC in the single year and to make a corresponding adjustment for each year of the NDC implementation period equal to the total amount of ITMOs that it transfers and acquires in each year of the NDC implementation period.

Option D {*averaging, including average per cooperative approach*}

Option D1 {*where the corresponding adjustment is for creation, first transfer and use*}

75.   A Party to calculate the average quantity of ITMOs that it creates, first transfers and uses towards achievement of its NDC by dividing the total ITMOs by the number of years of the NDC implementation period, including after averaging per cooperative approach, if applicable. The Party to then make a corresponding adjustment for the average amount of ITMOs in the single year of its NDC.

Option D2 {*where the corresponding adjustment is for transfer and acquisition*}

76.   A Party to calculate the average quantity of ITMOs that it transfers and acquires by dividing the total ITMOs by the number of years of the NDC implementation period, including after averaging per cooperative approach, if applicable. The Party to then make a corresponding adjustment for the average amount of ITMOs in the single year of its NDC.

Option E {*representative corresponding adjustments*}

Option E1 {*where the corresponding adjustment is for creation, first transfer and use*}

77.   A Party to identify all ITMOs that it creates, first transfers and uses towards achievement of its NDC and make a corresponding adjustment in the single year for an amount that is representative of the amount of ITMOs created, first transferred and used towards achievement of its NDC.

SBSTA48.Informal.2

Option E2 {*where the corresponding adjustment is for transfer and acquisition*}

78.   A Party to identify all ITMOs that it transfers and acquires in each year of its NDC implementation period and make a corresponding adjustment in the single year for an amount that is representative of the amount of ITMOs that it transfers and acquires in each year of its NDC implementation period.

Option F {*reporting in accordance with this guidance, periodically*}

Option F1 {*where the corresponding adjustment is for creation, first transfer and use*}

79.   A Party to make a corresponding adjustment for all ITMOs that it creates, first transfers and uses towards achievement of its NDC in accordance with the reporting requirements in this guidance.

Option F2 {*where the corresponding adjustment is for transfer and acquisition*}

80.   A Party to make a corresponding adjustment for all ITMOs that it transfers and acquires in accordance with the reporting requirements of this guidance.

Option G {*no specific guidance*}

{*no text required*}

D.   Multi-year nationally determined contributions

81.   A Party with a multi-year NDC to make a corresponding adjustment for the total amount of ITMOs:

(a)   Created, first transferred and used towards achievement of its NDC over the NDC period {*where the corresponding adjustment is for creation, first transfer and use*};

(b)   Transferred and acquired over the NDC period {*where the corresponding adjustment is for transfer and acquisition*}.

E.   Pre-2020 units/internationally transferred mitigation outcomes {*further development may be required for implementation*}

82.   In respect of pre-2020 units/ITMOs:

Option A {*use of pre-2020 units/ITMOs, corresponding adjustment for creating and using Party*}

(a)   where a Party is using pre-2020 units/ITMOs towards achievement of its NDC, both the creating Party and the using Party to make a corresponding adjustment in accordance with section X (Corresponding adjustment) {*further development may be required for implementation*}.

Option B {*use of pre-2020 units/ITMOs, corresponding adjustment only for using Party*}

(b)   the Party using pre-2020 units/ITMOs towards achievement of its NDC to make a corresponding adjustment in accordance with section X (Corresponding adjustment).

Option C {*no use of pre-2020 units*}

(c)   no Party to use pre-2020 units/ITMOs towards achievement of its NDC.

XIII.   Application of this guidance to emission reductions certified under the mechanism established by Article 6, paragraph 4

Option A {*guidance applicable to all emission reductions transferred internationally*}

83.   Section X (Corresponding adjustment) of this guidance applies to all emissions reductions under the mechanism established by Article 6, paragraph 4, when transferred internationally.

Option B {*guidance applicable where emission reductions from sectors/greenhouse gases are covered by the NDC*}

84.   Section X (Corresponding adjustment) of this guidance applies to emission reductions under the mechanism established by Article 6, paragraph 4, that result from a mitigation activity that is included in the sectors/greenhouse gases covered by the host Party's NDC, when those emission reductions are transferred internationally.

85.   This guidance not to apply to emission reductions under the mechanism established by Article 6, paragraph 4, if the mitigation activity is not included in the sectors/greenhouse gases covered by the host Party's NDC.

Option C {*forwarding based*}

86.   This guidance is not applicable to the initial forwarding of certified emission reductions from the Article 6, paragraph 4, mechanism registry.

87.   Section X (Corresponding adjustment) of this guidance to apply to any subsequent international transfer of certified emission reductions between registries/national accounts in the multilateral registry.

Option D {*national allowances-based*}

88.   This guidance to apply to emission reductions issued under the mechanism established by Article 6, paragraph 4. A Party with an absolute emission limitation or reduction target in its NDC may then transfer an equivalent quantity of national allowances {*further development may be required for implementation*}.

XIV.   Infrastructure

A.   Registry requirements

Option A {*registries*} {*further development may be required for implementation*} {*potential list below*}

89.   Each participating Party to have or have access to a registry that meets the requirements of this guidance.

90.   Each participating Party to ensure that its registry is capable of {*further potential list below*}:

(a)   Creating and, where applicable, issuing ITMOs/units;

(b)   Determining a unique serial number for each ITMO/unit;

(c)   First transfer of ITMOs/units;

(d)   Subsequent transfer of ITMOs/units;

(e)   Acquiring ITMO/units;

(f)   Demonstrating that ITMOs/units have been used towards achievement of an NDC (e.g. through cancelling or retiring ITMOs);

(g)   Ensuring the avoidance of double counting.

Option A1 {*no further requirements in relation to registry beyond Option A*}

{*no further text required*}

Option A2 {*all potential elements of Option A, plus all further elements below*}

91.   Each registry to have the following national accounts: issuance, holding, transfer, acquisition, cancellation, retirement and share of proceeds.

92.   The secretariat to maintain a multilateral registry for Parties that do not have a registry or do not have access to a registry.

93.   The secretariat to ensure the multilateral registry is capable of providing national accounts for issuance, holding, transfer, acquisition, cancellation, retirement and share of proceeds.

Option B {*distributed ledger*}

94.   Each participating Party to have or have access to a distributed ledger that meets the requirements of this guidance.

Option C {*no guidance required as no registry/registries or distributed ledger required as reporting is the basis for tracking ITMOs/units*}

{*no text required*}

B.   International transaction log/centralized accounting database/distributed ledger

Option A {*international transaction log*}

95.   The secretariat to establish and maintain an international transaction log capable of recording the following {*further development may be required for implementation*}.

96.   Each participating Party to ensure that its registry is capable of connection to the international transaction log.

Option B {*centralized accounting database*}

97.   The secretariat to establish and maintain a centralized accounting database to record summaries of transfers, acquisitions and holdings {*further development may be required for implementation*}.

Option C {*distributed ledger*}

98.   The secretariat/X to establish and maintain a distributed ledger that is accessible to all participating Parties {*further development may be required for implementation*}.

Option D {*no guidance required as no such infrastructure required, as reporting required*}

{*no text required*}

XV.   Safeguards

A.   Overall mitigation in global emissions

Option A {*cancellation-based*}

99.   The creating Party to make a corresponding adjustment for the full amount of ITMOs to be first transferred and the creating Party to cancel X per cent of the total amount of ITMOs prior to the first transfer and/or the using Party to cancel X per cent of the acquired ITMOs before use. The cancelled ITMOs not to be used by any Party towards achievement of its NDC.

Option B {*discounting-based*}

100.   The creating Party to make a corresponding adjustment for the full amount of ITMOs to be first transferred and the creating Party to discount by X per cent at the point of first transfer. The using Party to discount by X per cent the total quantity of ITMOs acquired prior to use towards achievement of its NDC. The discounted ITMOs not to be used by any Party towards achievement of its NDC.

Option C {*no overall mitigation in global mitigation requirement*}

{*no text required*}

B.   Uses for purposes other than towards achievement of nationally determined contributions

101.   An ITMO not to be used towards achievement of an NDC where it has been or is intended to be used {*potential list below*}:

(a)   Towards international mitigation action outside the UNFCCC;

(b)   Towards voluntary climate actions that are not mandatory in the relevant jurisdiction;

(c)   As a means of demonstrating climate finance provided pursuant to Article 9.

102.   Parties to make a corresponding adjustment for ITMOs used for purposes other than towards achievement of NDCs consistent with:

Option A {*make a corresponding adjustment for all as per this guidance*}

(a)   section X (Corresponding adjustment) {*further development may be required for implementation*};

Option B {*only make a corresponding adjustment where from within NDC*}

(b)   section X (Corresponding adjustment), where the ITMOs are from the sectors/greenhouse gases covered by the NDC.

{*further development may be required for implementation, for example, reference to double counting*}

C.   Limits

1.   Limits on creation and first transfer

Option A {*limits on creation, transfer and acquisition*} {*potential list below*}

103.   A Party to create and first transfer ITMOs in a manner that avoids fluctuations in the prices and quantities available in the international market for ITMOs {*further development may be required for implementation*}.

104.   A Party not to create or first transfer ITMOs where the ITMOs have been achieved in sectors that have a high degree of uncertainty {*further development may be required for implementation*}.

105.   A Party not to first transfer any quantity of ITMOs over the reporting period/NDC implementation period that is greater than X per cent of its quantified budget of allowable emissions for that reporting period/NDC implementation period.

106.   A Party to maintain a holding balance equal to X per cent of its mitigation target for that reporting period/NDC implementation period throughout the reporting period/NDC implementation period.

107.   A Party to maintain a minimum level of allowable emissions in the NDC time frame reserve.

108.   A Party's balance for the reporting period/NDC implementation period to not exceed X per cent of its actual emissions and to not exceed emission levels for the reporting period/NDC implementation period that are consistent with NDC achievement.

109.   A Party to not participate in the following types of transfers: {*further development may be required for implementation*}.

110.   An ITMO may be transferred only once.

111.   A Party to ensure that there is no secondary trading of ITMOs and that speculative trading is avoided {*further development may be required for implementation*}.

Option B {*no limits on creation, transfer or acquisition*}

{*no text required*}

2.   Limits on use towards achievement of nationally determined contributions

Option A {*limits on use*} {*potential list below*}

112.   A Party's use of ITMOs towards achievement of its NDC to be supplemental to domestic action and domestic action to constitute a significant element of the effort made by each Party towards achievement of its NDC.

113.   A Party not to use any quantity of ITMOs towards achievement of its NDC that is greater than X per cent of the actual emissions of that Party calculated for the reporting period/NDC implementation period.

114.   A Party not to use towards achievement of its NDC any ITMOs that were achieved in the period X {*further development may be needed for implementation, including specifying the years*}.

115.   A Party not to use pre-2020 units/ITMOs towards achievement of its NDC {*further development may be required for implementation*}.

116.   A Party not to bank/carry over ITMOs exceeding X from one reporting period/NDC implementation period to a subsequent reporting period/NDC implementation period {*further development may be required for implementation*}.

117.   A Party may carry over a quantity of ITMOs achieved in one reporting period/NDC implementation period to a subsequent reporting period/NDC implementation period equal to a maximum of X per cent of the actual emissions calculated for the reporting period/NDC implementation period {*further development may be required for implementation*}.

118.   An ITMO to only be used by a Party towards achievement of its NDC or voluntarily cancelled.

Option B {*no limits on use*}

{*no text required*}

XVI.   Share of proceeds for adaptation

Option A {*share of proceeds*}

119.   A share of proceeds from cooperative approaches to be used to assist developing country Parties that are particularly vulnerable to the adverse effects of climate change to meet the costs of adaptation.

120.   The share of proceeds to be collected in respect of:

Option A1 {*where activities are similar to Article 6, paragraph 4 mitigation activities*}

(a)   cooperative approaches that are baseline and crediting approaches that are similar to mitigation activities under the mechanism established by Article 6 paragraph 4;

Option A2 {*crediting approaches*}

(b)   crediting approaches implemented by Parties.

{*end of Option A2*}

121.   The share of proceeds to be set at {*potential list below*}:

(a) X per cent/5 per cent/an increasing per cent/a diminishing per cent of the amount of ITMOs transferred/used towards achievement of an NDC;

(b)   Consistent with the share of proceeds pursuant to Article 6, paragraph 6, for the mechanism established by Article 6, paragraph 4.

122.   The share of proceeds to be:

(a)   Collected by the creating/issuing Party at the first international transfer of ITMOs and/or collected by a Party using ITMOs towards achievement of its NDC;

(b)   Transferred by the Party to the Adaptation Fund.

Option B {*no share of proceeds*}

{*no text required*}

XVII.   Adaptation ambition {*further development may be required for implementation*}

123.   Mitigation co-benefits of adaptation action, including economic diversification {*further development may be required for implementation*}.

SBSTA.48.Informal.2

XVIII. Addressing negative social and economic impacts, Article 4, paragraph 15 {*further development may be required for implementation*}

XIX. Mitigation co-benefits resulting from Parties' adaptation actions and/or economic diversification plans {*further development may be required for implementation*}

XX. Multilateral governance and rules-based system {*further development may be required for implementation*}

———————

Framework Convention on
Climate Change

SBSTA48.Informal.3

Subsidiary Body for Scientific and Technological Advice
Forty-eighth session
Bonn, 30 April to 10 May 2018

16 March 2018

Informal document containing the draft elements of the rules, modalities and procedures for the mechanism established by Article 6, paragraph 4, of the Paris Agreement

Informal document by the Chair

Contents

SBSTA48.Informal.3

SBSTA48.Informal.3

Introduction

A.   Mandate

1.   Article 6, paragraph 4, of the Paris Agreement establishes a mechanism to contribute to the mitigation of greenhouse gas emissions and support sustainable development (hereinafter referred to as the mechanism). By decision 1/CP.21, paragraph 38, the Conference of the Parties requested the Subsidiary Body for Scientific and Technological Advice (SBSTA) to develop and recommend rules, modalities and procedures for the mechanism for adoption by the Conference of the Parties serving as the meeting of the Parties to the Paris Agreement (CMA) at its first session.

2.   At SBSTA 47, to facilitate the deliberations at SBSTA 48, the SBSTA requested the SBSTA Chair to prepare an informal document containing draft elements of the rules, modalities and procedures for the mechanism based on prior submissions by Parties under this agenda sub-item and the third iteration of the informal note prepared by the co-chairs of the relevant agenda item[1] (hereinafter referred to as the third iteration note).

B.   Scope

3.   The annex to this informal document contains the draft elements of the rules, modalities and procedures prepared by the SBSTA Chair on the basis of the above mandate (hereinafter referred to as the draft elements of the RMP).

C.   Approach

4.   The SBSTA Chair has developed the draft elements of the RMP on the basis of the third iteration note and previous submissions by the Parties under this agenda sub-item.

5.   The draft elements of the RMP have, in relation to the third iteration note, sought to:

(a)   Streamline the structure, including removing duplication, without removing elements;

(b)   Bring the aspects of each issue together to facilitate discussions at SBSTA 48;

(c)   Develop the language for the implementation of elements from the third iteration note, without developing full text;

(d)   Clarify options and the potential further elements to be considered.

6.   In the draft elements of the RMP, all paragraphs and sub-paragraphs have been numbered sequentially to make it easier for Parties to identify substantive content of the options when using the informal document to facilitate discussions at SBSTA 48.

7.   Generally, throughout the draft elements of the RMP, curly brackets containing italicized text, as in {*curly brackets containing italicized text*} are used to provide information about the relevant element.

8.   Where the draft elements of the RMP contain options, these are labelled as "**Option A**", "**Option B**", etc. To assist navigation of the text, options are followed by a brief indicative narrative, in curly brackets and in bold, italicized text ("{***narrative of the option***}"). Where, within a section of the draft elements of the RMP, the end of the last option in a group of options is followed by other elements that are not part of those options, the phrase "{*end of Option X*}" is inserted for clarity. No options extend beyond a section into the next section.

9.   Where an element/option has several potential sub-elements, the note "{*potential list below*}" is included just before the list begins, in order to show Parties that they need to consider each sub-element independently and not as a group of sub-elements. The note "{*further potential list below*}"

---

[1]   http://unfccc.int/cooperation_support/cooperative_implementation/items/9644.php and
http://unfccc.int/documentation/documents/advanced_search/items/6911.php?priref=600009936.

is used in a similar manner for sub-sub-elements. That note is not used where the sub-elements are a suite and are needed together.

10.   Where it appears that further development of a potential element or an option would be required for implementation, the following note is made: "{*further development may be required for implementation*}". In some cases, further possible actions or examples are provided to help Parties identify what further development might include.

11.   Where alternatives or choices may be selected within a sentence, a forward slash ("/") is used to indicate those alternatives so that the sentence remains readable as a whole. However, where there is "and/or", this means "and" as well as "or".

12.   Where there is provision for a certain number of events to be organised, members to be appointed, etc. the draft elements of the RMP use "*X*", "*Y*", "*Z*" etc. to indicate choices that would need to be taken.

13.   The selection of certain options may have implications on other options in other sections of the draft elements of the RMP. In order to keep the document manageable, not all consequential implications for other parts of the draft elements of the RMP are indicated. In certain cases, some options are incompatible with some other options in other sections and, where this is particularly acute, the draft elements of the RMP identify that in curly brackets.

14.   Furthermore, the draft elements of the RMP cannot assess all the possible ways in which options found in different parts of the text might be combined.

15.   There is a technical interconnection between these draft elements of the RMP and the draft elements of guidance for cooperative approaches referred to in Article 6, paragraph 2 of the Paris Agreement, as set out in informal document SBSTA 48.Informal.2.

16.   The draft elements of the RMP use the phrase "**A6.4ER**" to refer to emission reductions verified and certified under the mechanism, solely for the purposes of keeping the draft elements of the RMP short and readable (and without prejudice to its definition at a later stage by the SBSTA).

D.   Possible actions by the Subsidiary Body for Scientific and Technological Advice

17.   The SBSTA may wish to consider this informal document, and refine and elaborate the draft elements of the RMP contained herein.

Annex

Draft elements of the rules, modalities and procedures for the mechanism established by Article 6, paragraph 4, of the Paris Agreement

I. Preamble

Option A {*list of preambular paragraphs, including principles*}

{*see section II, Option A (Principles), below for list of potential principles*}

Option B {*no list of preambular paragraphs*}

{*no text is required*}

II. Principles

Option A {*list of principles*}

1.   The following principles to guide the implementation of the mechanism established by Article 6, paragraph 4, of the Paris Agreement[1] (hereinafter referred to as the mechanism) {*potential list below*}:

(a)   The mechanism to contribute to the objectives of the Paris Agreement as referred to in its Article 2;

(b)   In accordance with Article 6, paragraph 4(a), the mechanism to aim to promote the mitigation of greenhouse gas emissions while fostering sustainable development;

(c)   In accordance with Article 6, paragraph 4(b), the mechanism to aim to incentivize and facilitate participation in the mitigation of greenhouse gas emissions by public and private entities authorized by a Party;

(d)   Pursuant to the aim set out in Article 6, paragraph 4(b), the mechanism to aim to incentivize and facilitate the long-term engagement in the mechanism of Parties and public and private entities authorized by them;

(e)   In accordance with Article 6, paragraph 4(c), the mechanism to aim to contribute to the reduction of emission levels in the host Party, which will benefit from mitigation activities resulting in emission reductions that can also be used by another Party to fulfil its nationally determined contribution (NDC);

(f)   In accordance with Article 6, paragraph 4(d), the mechanism to aim to deliver an overall mitigation in global emissions;

(g)   Pursuant to the preamble to the Paris Agreement, the mechanism to respect, promote and consider Parties' respective obligations on human rights;

(h)   Pursuant to Article 3, the mechanism should support the progression of each participating Party's efforts over time;

(i)   Pursuant to Article 4, paragraph 3, the mechanism should support progression in successive NDCs of participating Parties;

(j)   Pursuant to Article 4, paragraph 15, Parties to take into consideration the concerns of Parties with economies most affected by the impacts of response measures, particularly developing country Parties, when participating in the mechanism;

(k)   The mechanism and its rules, modalities and procedures to ensure the environmental integrity of the mechanism;

---

[1] References to "Article" are to articles of the Paris Agreement, unless otherwise specified.

(l)   The mechanism allows for higher ambition of participating Parties in their mitigation and adaptation actions;

(m)   The mechanism to ensure that participation by a Party, and any public or private entities authorized by it, in the mechanism is consistent with the mitigation objectives of that Party;

(n)   The mechanism to ensure consistency with Article 3 and Article 4, paragraphs 3 and 4, including by preventing perverse incentives for not progressing towards economy-wide targets and not progressing beyond the Party's then current NDC;

(o)   The mechanism to prevent perverse incentives for participating Parties not to authorize mitigation activities that deliver real, measurable and long-term benefits and emission reductions that are additional;

(p)   The mechanism to prevent perverse incentives for participating Parties not to engage in a manner that is consistent over the long term and that provides predictability and a stable investment signal for public and private entities participating in the mechanism;

(q)   Participating Parties to avoid unilateral measures that constitute a means of arbitrary or unjustifiable discrimination or a disguised restriction on international trade;

(r)   The implementation of the mechanism to be transparent;

(s)   Any Party may voluntarily participate in the mechanism, notwithstanding the nature of its NDC;

(t)   All types of mitigation activity may be considered for registration under the mechanism.

Option B {*no principles*}

{*no text is required*}

III.   Definitions

2.   For the purpose of the rules, modalities and procedures for the mechanism, the definitions contained in Article 1 and the provisions of Article 17 to apply. Furthermore:

(a)   A mitigation activity is "**additional**" under the mechanism if it meets the requirements in section XII.D below (Additionality);

(b)   An "**Article 6, paragraph 4, activity**" is an activity that meets the requirements in Article 6, paragraphs 4–6, these rules, modalities and procedures and any further decisions of the Conference of the Parties serving as the meeting of the Parties to the Paris Agreement (CMA);

(c)   An "**Article 6, paragraph 4, emission reduction**" (hereinafter referred to as an **A6.4ER**) is a unit that is issued pursuant to Article 6, paragraphs 4–7 and these rules, modalities and procedures;

(d)   The "**mechanism registry**" means the registry established under section VII below mechanism registry);

(e)   A "**certified emission reduction**" (**CER**) is a unit issued pursuant to Article 12 of the Kyoto Protocol and the requirements thereunder, as well as the relevant provisions in the annex to decision 3/CMP.1, and is equal to one metric tonne of carbon dioxide equivalent, calculated using global warming potentials defined in decision 2/CP.3 or as subsequently revised in accordance with Article 5 of the Kyoto Protocol {*further development may be required for implementation, as there are other modalities and procedures for the CDM for other project types*};

(f)   An "**emission reduction unit**" (**ERU**) is a unit issued pursuant to the relevant provisions in the annex to decision 13/CMP.1 and is equal to one metric tonne of carbon dioxide equivalent, calculated using global warming potentials defined in decision 2/CP.3 or as subsequently revised in accordance with Article 5 of the Kyoto Protocol;

(g)   "**Global stakeholders**" means the public, including individuals, groups or communities, affected or likely to be affected by an Article 6, paragraph 4, activity, irrespective of their location;

SBSTA48.Informal.3

(h)   "**Local stakeholders**" means the public, including individuals, groups or communities, affected or likely to be affected by an Article 6, paragraph 4, activity as a result of their vicinity to the activity;

(i)   A "**nationally determined contribution limitation quotient unit**" is a unit issued pursuant to the relevant provisions under this decision and is equal to one metric tonne of carbon dioxide equivalent, calculated using approved global warming potentials {*further development may be required for implementation*};

(j)   A "**registry**" has the meaning given to it in the guidance for cooperative approaches referred to in Article 6, paragraph 2;

(k)   An "**overall mitigation in global emissions**" takes place when emission reductions are delivered at a level that goes beyond what would be achieved through the delivery of the host Party's NDC and the acquiring Party's NDC in aggregate;

(l)   "**Own mitigation benefit**" occurs when the amount of A6.4ERs issued for a mitigation activity is lower than the verified emission reductions achieved by the mitigation activity {*further development may be required for implementation*};

(m)   The "**Supervisory Body**" is the body designated by the CMA in accordance with Article 6, paragraph 4, to supervise the mechanism under the authority and guidance of the CMA.

IV. Scope and purpose

A. Scopes of activities

3.   The following mitigation is included within the scope of the mechanism: {*potential list below*} {*further development may be required for implementation*}:

(a)   Emission reductions;

(b)   Emission removals;

(c)   Emissions avoided;

(d)   A full spectrum of mitigation activities, including mitigation co-benefits of adaptation actions and/or economic diversification plans;

4.   The following types of mitigation activity may be registered as Article 6, paragraph 4, activities {*potential list below*} {*further development may be required for implementation*}:

(a)   Projects;

(b)   Programmes of activities;

(c)   Sectoral approaches;

(d)   Other types approved by the Supervisory Body;

(e)   Activities under non-UNFCCC programmes.

5.   An A6.4ER issued to be {*potential list below*}:

(a)   Equal to one metric tonne of carbon dioxide equivalent;

(b)   Measured in a metric other than tonnes of carbon dioxide equivalent;

6.   An A6.4ER to be calculated {*potential list below*}:

(a)   In accordance with the methodologies and common metrics assessed by the IPCC and adopted by the COP/CMA;

(b)   Using global warming potentials assessed/recommended by the IPCC and adopted by the COP/CMA;

7.   An A6.4ER to be issued in respect of mitigation:

Option A {*achieved on or after 1 January 2020*}

(a)   Achieved on or after 1 January 2020

Option B {*no time limitation*}

{*no text required*}

B.   Scope of rules, modalities and procedures

Option A {*special circumstances of LDCs and SIDS*}

8.   In relation to the least developed countries and small island developing States, the special circumstances of the least developed countries and small island developing States as set out in Article 4, paragraph 6, to be recognized where these rules, modalities and procedures relate to NDCs {*further development may be required for implementation*}.

Option B {*no special circumstances*}

{*no text is required*}

C.   Purpose of rules, modalities and procedures {*further development may be required for implementation*}

9.   The purpose of these rules, modalities and procedures is to set out {*potential list below*}:

(a)   Key requirements and processes for the operation of the mechanism;

(b)   How each Party may use emission reductions resulting from Article 6, paragraph 4, activities towards achievement of its NDC pursuant to Article 6, paragraphs 4(b) and 5.

V.   Role of the Conference of the Parties serving as the meeting of the Parties to the Paris Agreement

10.   The CMA to have authority over and provide guidance on the mechanism.

11.   The CMA to provide guidance to the Supervisory Body by taking decisions on {*potential list below*}:

(a)   The recommendations made by the Supervisory Body on its rules of procedure;

(b)   The recommendations made by the Supervisory Body in accordance with these rules, modalities and procedures and relevant decisions of the CMA;

(c)   Any matters relating to the operation of the mechanism, as appropriate.

12.   The CMA to review these rules, modalities and procedures periodically/ by no later than {*X date*}, on the basis of recommendations from X {*further development may be required for implementation*}.

VI.   Supervisory Body

A.   Membership

13.   The Supervisory Body to comprise X members from Parties to the Paris Agreement, as follows, ensuring gender-balanced representation and technical competence:

Option A {*CDM EB model*} {*below text is taken from decision 3/CMP.1, annex, paragraph 7*}

(a)   One member from each of the five United Nations regional groups;

(b)   Two other members from the Parties included in Annex I;

(c)   Two other members from the Parties not included in Annex I;

(d)   One representative of the small island developing States.

Option B {*JISC model*} {*below text is taken from decision 9/CMP.1, annex, paragraph 4*}

(a)   Three members from Parties included in Annex I that are undergoing the process of transition to a market economy;

(b)   Three members from Parties included in Annex I not referred to in subparagraph (a) above;

(c)   Three members from Parties not included in Annex I;

(d)   One member from the small island developing States.

Option C {*new model*} {*potential list below*}

(a)   Ensuring balanced representation of Parties:

    (i) X members from each of the five United Nations regional groups;

    (ii) X members from developed country Parties;

    (iii) X members from developing country Parties, including X members from the least developed country Parties and X members from small island developing States;

(b) X members from private sector organizations or non-governmental organizations.

{*end of Option C*}

14.   The CMA to elect, on the basis of nominations by the relevant UN regional groups and other constituency groups:

Option A {*members only*}

(a)   members of the Supervisory Body.

Option B {*members and alternate members*}

(b)   members and an alternate for each member of the Supervisory Body.

B.   Rules of procedure

15.   The Supervisory Body to develop its draft rules of procedure addressing, inter alia, the following areas, for consideration and adoption at CMA X {*potential list below*}:

(a)   Membership issues, including nomination, election, acting in personal capacity, duration, resignation, suspension and termination of membership, filling vacant seats, and covering costs;

(b)   Safeguarding against conflicts of interest and ensuring confidentiality;

(c)   Quorum and voting rules;

(d)   Transparency of meetings and their documentation.

16.   The Supervisory Body to develop its draft rules of procedure drawing on:

Option A {*draw from CDM EB*}

(a)   the rules of procedure of the Executive Board of the clean development mechanism.

Option B {*draw from JISC*}

(b)   the rules of procedure of the Joint Implementation Supervisory Committee.

Option C {*new body*}

{*no text is required*}

C.   Governance and functions

Option A {*centralized system*}

17.   In accordance with Article 6, paragraph 4, the Supervisory Body to supervise the mechanism, under the authority and guidance of the CMA, and be accountable to the CMA. In this context, the Supervisory Body to {*potential list below*}:

(a)   Develop the requirements and processes necessary to operationalize the mechanism, including by:

(i)   Developing requirements for accrediting operational entities;

(ii)   Developing requirements that ensure that the registration of mitigation activities as Article 6, paragraph 4, activities and the issuance of A6.4ERs are in accordance with these rules, modalities and procedures and relevant decisions of the CMA and the Supervisory Body;

(iii)   Developing baseline and monitoring methodologies and standardized baselines for Article 6, paragraph 4, activities, prioritizing the baseline and monitoring methodologies and standardized baselines that promote mitigation at scale;

(iv)   Developing the mechanism registry;

(b)   Operate the mechanism, including by:

(i)   Designating operational entities that meet the requirements for accreditation and managing their performance;

(ii)   Taking appropriate measures to promote the regional availability of designated operational entities;

(iii)   Registering mitigation activities as Article 6, paragraph 4, activities if they meet the requirements for registration;

(iv)   Approving the issuance of A6.4ERs for registered Article 6, paragraph 4, activities if the requirements for issuance have been met;

(v)   Forwarding/transferring A6.4ERs from the mechanism registry in accordance with procedures adopted by the Supervisory Body;

(vi)   Maintaining the mechanism registry;

(c)   Support the implementation of the mechanism and its transparency, including by:

(i)   Developing and maintaining a public registry of information related to proposed and registered Article 6, paragraph 4, activities, subject to confidentiality;

(ii)   Promoting public awareness of the mechanism, including on its role in implementing the Paris Agreement and NDCs;

(iii)   Making publicly available all requirements and related documentation for the mechanism.

18.   In exercising the functions referred to in paragraph 17 above, the Supervisory Body to {*potential list below*}:

(a)   Operate in an executive and supervisory manner, defining and developing the governance rules of the support structure, including panels and groups of technical experts as needed, delegating work to, and considering recommendations from, them;

(b)   Draw on experience gained with and lessons learned from joint implementation and the clean development mechanism under Articles 6 and 12, respectively, of the Kyoto Protocol.

19.   In exercising the functions referred to in paragraph 17 above, the Supervisory Body to also {*potential list below*}:

(a)   Report on its activities to the CMA at each of its sessions;

(b)   Make recommendations to the CMA on any amendments to the rules, modalities and procedures for the mechanism;

(c)   Seek guidance from the CMA on any matters relating to the operation of the mechanism;

(d)   Review Article 6, paragraph 4, activities and how the mechanism delivers an overall mitigation in global emissions, and report on the findings to the CMA.

Option B {*host Party led system*} and

Option C {*dual system (both centralized and host Party led)*}

20.   In accordance with Article 6, paragraph 4, the Supervisory Body to supervise the mechanism. In this context, the Supervisory Body to {*potential list below*}:

(a)   Carry out the functions and modalities referred to in paragraphs 17-19 above {*further development may be required for implementation to specify which of potential elements in Option A would apply*};

(b)   Develop international requirements and conformity assessment processes for Article 6, paragraph 4, activities;

(c)   Review the implementation of the national processes of each host Party for conformity with international requirements and periodically certify them {*further development may be required for implementation*};

(d)   Ensure that each Party applies the centralized or Party-led system consistently {*further development may be required for implementation*}.

D.   Role of the secretariat

21.   Pursuant to Article 17, the secretariat to serve the Supervisory Body. In this context, the secretariat to, inter alia {*further development may be required for implementation*}:

(a)   Support the operation of the mechanism, the Supervisory Body and its support structure;

(b)   Collect fees to cover the administrative costs of the Supervisory Body and its support structure;

(c)   Report to the CMA on overall mitigation in global emissions delivered through the mechanism;

(d)   Report to the CMA, at each of its sessions, on the collection of the share of proceeds levied in accordance with section XIV (Share of proceeds) below;

(e)   Report the following information: {*further development may be required for implementation, including possible reporting to the global stocktake under Article 14*}.

VII.   The mechanism registry

22.   The Supervisory Body to establish and maintain a registry for the mechanism (hereinafter referred to as the mechanism registry) {*further development may be required for implementation*}.

23.   The secretariat to serve as the registry administrator to maintain the mechanism registry under the authority of the Supervisory Body.

VIII.   Participation, benefits and responsibilities of host Parties

A.   Participation requirements for host Parties

Option A {*participation requirements*}

24.   A Party may participate on a voluntary basis in the mechanism by hosting Article 6, paragraph 4, activities if it meets the following requirements {*potential list below*}:

(a)   It is a Party to the Paris Agreement;

(b)   It has prepared, communicated and maintained successive NDCs and is currently maintaining an NDC in accordance with Article 4, paragraph 2, and relevant decisions of the CMA;

(c)   It complies with the requirements in Article 6, paragraphs 4 and 5;

(d)   It has designated a national authority for the mechanism and has communicated that designation to the secretariat;

(e)   It has a registry or has an account in the mechanism registry for holding A6.4ERs;

(f)   It submits national inventory reports in accordance with the modalities, procedures and guidelines adopted by the CMA pursuant to Article 13, paragraph 13;

(g)   It ensures that its hosting of Article 6, paragraph 4, activities and generation of A6.4ERs therefrom is guided by its domestic mitigation objectives;

(h)   Where applicable, it has in place national processes and institutional arrangements for hosting Article 6, paragraph 4, activities that have been certified by the Supervisory Body.

Option B {*application of Article 6.2 guidance participation requirements*}

25.   A Party may participate in Article 6, paragraph 4, activities if it meets the requirements for participating in cooperative approaches set out in the guidance for cooperative approaches referred to in Article 6 paragraph 2.

B.   Responsibilities of host Parties

Option A {*responsibilities of hosting Parties*}

26.   A Party hosting an Article 6, paragraph 4, activity to {*potential list below*}:

(a)   Provide confirmation to the Supervisory Body that participation by the Party and any participants in the proposed Article 6, paragraph 4, activity is voluntary;

(b)   Provide authorization to the Supervisory Body of the proposed Article 6, paragraph 4, activity;

(c)   Provide confirmation to the Supervisory Body that the proposed Article 6, paragraph 4, activity fosters sustainable development in the host Party;

(d)   Provide an explanation to the Supervisory Body as to how the proposed Article 6, paragraph 4, activity relates to the NDC of the host Party;

(e)   When authorizing the participation of public or private entities in the Article 6, paragraph 4, activity, provide authorization of that participation to the Supervisory Body;

(f)   Provide an explanation to the Supervisory Body as to how the proposed Article 6, paragraph 4, activity conforms to the implementation of the United Nations Sustainable Development Goals in the host Party;

(g)   Provide an explanation to the Supervisory Body as to how the proposed Article 6, paragraph 4, activity conforms to the host Party's obligations on human rights;

(h)   Provide an explanation to the Supervisory Body of the conditions under which it may withdraw its authorization of the proposed Article 6, paragraph 4, activity and/or withdraw its authorization of the participation of any public or private entities in the activity;

(i)   Provide confirmation to the Supervisory Body that local stakeholder consultation has been conducted for the proposed Article 6, paragraph 4, activity;

(j)   Provide confirmation to the Supervisory Body that the proposed Article 6, paragraph 4, activity respects the safeguards adopted by the Supervisory Body in relation to such activities;

(k)   Have provided, in accordance with the modalities, procedures and guidelines adopted by the CMA pursuant to Article 13, paragraph 13, information on all Article 6, paragraph 4, activities hosted by the Party and all A6.4ERs that the Party has internationally transferred or used towards achievement of its NDC;

    (l)   Where applicable, have national processes that conform to the international requirements developed by the Supervisory Body to operationalize the mechanism in its own jurisdiction and, following certification of those national processes by the Supervisory Body, have implemented them in accordance with these rules, modalities and procedures and relevant decisions of the CMA and/or the Supervisory Body {*relates to Options B and C in section VI.C (Supervisory Body, Governance and functions)*};

    (m)   Where applicable, have notified the Supervisory Body of national processes for the implementation of the mechanism in its jurisdiction, including authorization of and participation in mitigation activities, registration of mitigation activities as Article 6, paragraph 4, activities and enforcement of requirements {*relates to Options B and C in section VI.C (Supervisory Body, Governance and functions)*};

    (n)   Where applicable, provide a notification to the Supervisory Body of the registration of Article 6, paragraph 4, activities and the verification and certification of emission reductions {*relates to Options B and C in section VI.C (Supervisory Body, Governance and functions)*}.

Option B {*application of Article 6.2 guidance participation requirements*}

27.   A Party hosting Article 6, paragraph 4, activities to meet the requirements for participating in cooperative approaches set out in the guidance for cooperative approaches referred to in Article 6, paragraph 2.

C.   Benefits for host Parties

28.   A Party hosting Article 6, paragraph 4, activities to receive/ to aim to ensure the following benefits {*potential list below*}:

    (a)   Reduction of emissions in the host Party as a result of the implementation of Article 6, paragraph 4, activities;

    (b)   Fostering of sustainable development;

    (c)   Achievement of permanent and long-term benefits over periods that exceed the crediting periods of the Article 6, paragraph 4, activities;

    (d)   Enhancement of participation of public and private entities authorized by the host Party;

    (e)   Improvements over time of the regional distribution of Article 6, paragraph 4, activities;

    (f)   Capacity-building in relation to the implementation of Article 6, paragraph 4, activities.

D.   Addressing host-Party benefits

29.   A Party hosting Article 6, paragraph 4, activities to {*potential list below*}:

    (a)   Ensure coherence between its NDC and the host-Party benefits resulting from Article 6, paragraph 4, activities;

    (b)   Ensure coherence between its emissions and the host-Party benefits resulting from Article 6, paragraph 4, activities.

IX.   Participation and responsibilities of transferring, acquiring and using Parties

A.   Participation requirements for transferring, acquiring and using Parties

Option A {*participation requirements*}

30.   A Party may transfer and/or acquire A6.4ERs, and/or use A6.4ERs towards achievement of its NDC, if it meets the following requirements {*potential list below*}:

    (a)   It is a Party to the Paris Agreement;

(b)   It has prepared, communicated and maintained successive NDCs and is currently maintaining an NDC in accordance with Article 4, paragraph 2, and relevant decisions of the CMA;

(c)   If it has designated a national authority for the mechanism, it has communicated that designation to the secretariat;

(d)   It has a registry or has a Party account in the mechanism registry for holding A6.4ERs;

(e)   It submits national inventory reports and information relating to Article 6, paragraph 4 mechanism activities in accordance with the modalities, procedures and guidelines adopted by the CMA pursuant to Article 13, paragraph 13.

Option B {*application of Article 6.2 guidance participation requirements*}

31.   A Party may transfer or acquire A6.4ERs, and/or use A6.4ERs towards achievement of its NDC, if it meets the requirements for participating in cooperative approaches as set out in the guidance for cooperative approaches referred to in Article 6, paragraph 2.

B.   Responsibilities of transferring/acquiring Parties

Option A {*responsibilities of transferring/acquiring Parties*} {*potential list below*}

32.   A Party transferring or acquiring A6.4ERs to have provided, in accordance with the modalities, procedures and guidelines adopted by the CMA pursuant to Article 13, paragraph 13, information on all Article 6, paragraph 4, activities in which the Party is participating and all A6.4ERs that the Party has transferred or acquired.

Option B {*application of Article 6.2 guidance participation requirements*}

33.   A Party transferring or acquiring A6.4ERs to meet the requirements for participating in cooperative approaches as set out in the guidance for cooperative approaches referred to in Article 6, paragraph 2.

C.   Responsibilities of using Parties

Option A {*responsibilities of using Parties*}

34.   A Party using A6.4ERs towards achievement of its NDC to {*potential list below*}:

(a)   Provide confirmation to the Supervisory Body that participation by the Party and the participants in the proposed Article 6, paragraph 4, activity is voluntary;

(b)   When authorizing the participation of public or private entities in the Article 6, paragraph 4, activity, provide authorization of that participation to the Supervisory Body;

(c)   Provide confirmation to the Supervisory Body that the proposed Article 6, paragraph 4, activity fosters sustainable development in the participating Parties;

(d)   Provide an explanation to the Supervisory Body as to how the proposed Article 6, paragraph 4, activity conforms to the implementation of the United Nations Sustainable Development Goals in the participating Parties;

(e)   Provide an explanation to the Supervisory Body as to how the proposed Article 6, paragraph 4, activity and the use of A6.4ERs from the activity conforms to the Party's obligations on human rights;

(f)   Provide an explanation to the Supervisory Body of the conditions under which it may withdraw its authorization of the participation of any public or private entities in the activity, if such conditions exist;

(g)   Have provided, in accordance with the modalities, procedures and guidelines adopted by the CMA pursuant to Article 13, paragraph 13, information on all Article 6, paragraph 4, activities in which the Party is participating and all A6.4ERs that the Party has used towards achievement of its NDC.

Option B {*application of Article 6.2 guidance participation requirements*}

35.   A Party using A6.4ERs towards achievement of its NDC to meet the requirements for participating in cooperative approaches as set out in the guidance for cooperative approaches referred to in Article 6, paragraph 2.

X.   Participation by other actors

A.   Incentivizing and facilitating participation of public and private entities authorized by a Party {*potential list below*}

36.   Participating Parties to incentivize public and private entities to participate in Article 6, paragraph 4, activities in accordance with the provisions relating to the authorization of such participation {*further development may be required for implementation*}.

37.   Participation in Article 6, paragraph 4, activities by public and private entities and other non-State actors may include acquiring and transferring A6.4ERs and using A6.4ERs for purposes other than towards achievement of the NDC of a Party.

B.   Authorizing participation of public and private entities {*further development may be required for implementation*}

XI.   Designated operational entities

A.   Validation of mitigation activities

38.   A designated operational entity to independently evaluate a mitigation activity against the requirements set out in these rules, modalities and procedures, relevant decisions of the CMA and relevant requirements developed by the Supervisory Body (hereinafter referred to as validation) for:

(a)   Registration of the mitigation activity as an Article 6, paragraph 4, activity;

(b)   Other purposes as may be defined by the Supervisory Body.

B.   Verification and certification of emission reductions

39.   A designated operational entity to independently review and determine emission reductions that have occurred as a result of the implementation of an Article 6, paragraph 4, activity during the monitoring period (hereinafter referred to as verification) and provide written assurance of the emission reductions verified, for the issuance of A6.4ERs for the Article 6, paragraph 4, activity (hereinafter referred to as certification).

XII.   Eligible mitigation activities

A.   Mitigation activities in the context of the host Party's nationally determined contribution

Option A {*mitigation activities may be inside or outside the host Party's NDC*}

40.   Mitigation activities taking place in or outside the sectors/greenhouse gases/period covered by the NDC of the host Party may be registered as Article 6, paragraph 4, activities if they meet the requirements of these rules, modalities and procedures and relevant decisions of the CMA and the Supervisory Body.

Option B {*mitigation activities may only be inside the host Party's NDC*}

Option B1 {*applies to all Parties*}

41.   Only mitigation activities that are in the sectors/greenhouse gases/period covered by the NDC of the host Party and meet the requirements of these rules, modalities and procedures and other decisions of the CMA and the Supervisory Body may be registered as Article 6, paragraph 4, activities.

Option B2 {*does not apply to all Parties – special circumstances of the LDCs and SIDS recognized*}

42.   Only mitigation activities that are in the sectors/greenhouse gases/period covered by the NDC of the host Party and meet the requirements of these rules, modalities and procedures and relevant decisions of the CMA and the Supervisory Body may be registered as Article 6, paragraph 4, activities.

43.   For Parties that are least developed countries or small island developing States, any mitigation activities may be registered as Article 6, paragraph 4, activities if they meet the requirements of these rules, modalities and procedures and relevant decisions of the CMA and the Supervisory Body.

Option C {*mitigation activities may only be outside the host Party's NDC*}

44.   Only mitigation activities that are outside the greenhouse gases/sectors/period covered by the NDC of the host Party and meet the requirements of these rules, modalities and procedures and relevant decisions of the CMA and the Supervisory Body may be registered as Article 6, paragraph 4, activities.

Option D {*no specification on whether they may be within or outside the host Party's NDC*}

{*no text is required*}

B.   General requirements for mitigation activities

45.   An Article 6, paragraph 4, activity to {*potential list below*}:

(a)   Deliver real, measurable and long-term benefits related to the mitigation of climate change;

(b)   Apply a crediting period approved by the Supervisory Body;

(c)   Deliver permanent emission reductions and avoid and/or require correction of reversals;

(d)   Avoid incentivizing the use of technologies in a manner that disincentivizes the uptake of newer, more environmentally friendly and/or less greenhouse gas intensive technologies;

(e)   Foster sustainable development in accordance with Article 6, paragraph 4(a);

(f)   Include local stakeholder consultation;

(g)   Not include activity types that have negative environmental impacts;

(h)   Foster transition towards a low-carbon economy, in accordance with the long-term low-emission development strategies of the participating Parties communicated in accordance with Article 4, paragraph 19;

(i)   Be authorized by the host Party pursuant to decision 1/CP.21, paragraph 37(a).

C.   Baseline approach

46.   An Article 6, paragraph 4, activity to apply one or more of the following approaches to setting the baseline and calculating emission reductions achieved by the activity in accordance with the methodology approved by the Supervisory Body {*potential list below*}:

(a)   Application of a dynamic baseline that is updated upon changes to the assumptions for setting the baseline or is automatically updated;

(b)   Application of a conservative baseline that is below 'business as usual' and applies best available technologies;

(c)   Application of a baseline that reflects all relevant national and sectoral policies of the host Party and is updated at the point of changes to those national and sectoral policies;

(d)   Application of a baseline and monitoring methodology that takes into account any net leakage due to the implementation of the activity;

(e)   Application of conservative default factors and/or higher default factors for the calculation of emission reductions.

D.   Additionality

47.   An Article 6, paragraph 4, activity to be additional by demonstrating that:

Option A {*reference to what would otherwise have occurred*}

(a)   Emissions are reduced below those that would have occurred in the absence of the activity.

Option B {*definition related to activity being beyond the NDC*}

(b)   The reduction of emissions goes beyond what would be achieved through the delivery of the NDCs of the host Party {*further development may be required for implementation*}.

Option C {*definition linked to scope of NDC*}

(c)   {*further development may be required for implementation*}.

XIII.   Mitigation activity cycle

A.   Design

48.   To develop a mitigation activity as an Article 6, paragraph 4, activity, the activity to be designed to meet the requirements in these rules, modalities and procedures and any other relevant requirements defined by the CMA and the Supervisory Body.

B.   Validation

49.   The proposed mitigation activity to be validated by a designated operational entity in accordance with the relevant validation requirements adopted by the Supervisory Body.

C.   Registration

50.   After a positive validation, the design of the activity and the validation outcome to be submitted to the Supervisory Body, in accordance with the relevant requirements developed by the Supervisory Body.

51.   The mitigation activity to be registered as an Article 6, paragraph 4, activity if the Supervisory Body decides that the design of the mitigation activity and the validation meet the relevant requirements developed by the Supervisory Body.

D.   Monitoring {*further development may be required for implementation*}

52.   Monitoring of emission reductions achieved by a registered Article 6, paragraph 4, activity to be in accordance with the relevant requirements developed by the Supervisory Body.

E.   Verification and certification {*further development may be required for implementation*}

53.   The monitoring of the emission reductions to be verified and certified by a designated operational entity in accordance with the relevant requirements developed by the Supervisory Body.

F.   Issuance {*further development may be required for implementation*} {*potential list below*}

54.   For the issuance of A6.4ERs, the verification and certification to be submitted to the Supervisory Body and be in accordance with the relevant requirements developed by the Supervisory Body.

55.   The Supervisory Body to approve the issuance of A6.4ERs if it decides that the verification and certification meet the relevant requirements developed by the Supervisory Body.

56.   The registry administrator to, in accordance with section VII (The mechanism registry) and the relevant requirements developed by the Supervisory Body, issue the A6.4ERs into

Option A {*issuance into the mechanism registry*}

(a)   the mechanism registry.

Option B {*issuance into a registry*}

(b)   the relevant registry {*further development may be required for implementation*}.

G.   Forwarding/transfer from the mechanism registry {*further development may be required for implementation, in coordination with section XIV (Share of proceeds)*}

57.   The registry administrator to:

Option A {*unspecified destination of share of proceeds*}

(a)   Forward/transfer X per cent of the issued A6.4ERs to an account for assisting developing country Parties that are particularly vulnerable to the adverse effects of climate change to meet the costs of adaptation;

Option B {*specified destination of share of proceeds to Adaptation Fund*}

(b)   Forward/transfer X per cent of the issued A6.4ERs to an account held by the Adaptation Fund for assisting developing country Parties that are particularly vulnerable to the adverse effects of climate change to meet the costs of adaptation;

{*end of Option B*}

(c)   For the remaining issued A6.4ERs, forward/transfer the specified amount of A6.4ERs in accordance with the instructions of the participants in the Article 6, paragraph 4, activity, in accordance with the relevant requirements developed by the Supervisory Body.

H.   Voluntary cancellation

58.   The registry administrator to cancel the specified amount of A6.4ERs {*further development may be required for implementation, perhaps by delegation to develop requirements to the Supervisory Body*}.

I.   Grievance process/appeal rights

59.   Stakeholders, participants and participating Parties may appeal decisions of the Supervisory Body or request that a grievance be addressed by the Supervisory Body {*further development may be required for implementation, perhaps by delegation to develop requirements to the Supervisory Body to be endorsed by the CMA*}.

J.   Protection of human rights

60.   Stakeholders, participants and participating Parties may inform the Supervisory Body of alleged violations of human rights resulting from an Article 6, paragraph 4, activity {*further development may be required for implementation*}.

K.   Referral of matters to the committee referred to in Article 15

61.   Referral to the committee referred to in Article 15, paragraph 2, to be in accordance with its modalities and procedures {*further development may be required for implementation*}.

L.   Reporting

62.   Each participating Party to provide information on its registered Article 6, paragraph 4, activities and on issuance, transfer, acquisition of A6.4ERs and use of A6.4ERs towards achievement of its NDC in accordance with Article 13, paragraph 13.

XIV.   Levy of share of proceeds towards administration and adaptation

A.   Share of proceeds for adaptation (level and timing)

Option A {*unspecified destination of share of proceeds*}

63.   The share of proceeds from an Article 6, paragraph 4, activity that is levied to assist developing country Parties that are particularly vulnerable to the adverse effects of climate change to meet the costs of adaptation to be delivered to the relevant mechanism registry account {*further development may be required for implementation*}.

Option B {*specified destination of share of proceeds to Adaptation Fund*}

64.   The share of proceeds from an Article 6, paragraph 4, activity that is levied to assist developing country Parties that are particularly vulnerable to the adverse effects of climate change to meet the costs of adaptation to be delivered to the Adaption Fund.

{*end of Option B*}

65.   The share of proceeds to be set and levied at

Option A {*percentage at issuance*}

(a) X per cent/5 per cent at issuance.

Option B {*percentage at forwarding/first transfer*}

(b) X per cent/5 per cent at forwarding/first transfer.

Option C {*increasing rate over time at transfer*}

(c) X per cent/5 per cent at forwarding/first transfer, increasing by Y per cent at each subsequent transfer.

Option D {*linked with an overall mitigation in global emissions*}

{*further development may be required for implementation*}

B.   Share of proceeds for administrative expenses (level and timing)

66.   The share of proceeds from an Article 6, paragraph 4, activity that is levied to cover administrative expenses to be:

(a)   USD X, payable at the time of the request for registration;

(b)   USD X per A6.4ER issued for the activity, payable at the time of the request for issuance of A6.4ERs.

XV.   Delivering overall mitigation in global emissions

67.   The mechanism to deliver an overall mitigation in global emissions in accordance with this section.

Option A {*cancellation and/or discounting*}

Option A1 {*cancellation*}

(a)   The host Party to make a corresponding adjustment under the guidance for cooperative approaches referred to in Article 6, paragraph 2, for the full amount of A6.4ERs to be first transferred and the host Party to cancel X per cent of the total amount of A6.4 ERs prior to the first transfer and/or the using Party to cancel X per cent of the acquired A6.4ERs before use towards achievement of its NDC. The cancelled A6.4ERs not to be used by any Party towards achievement of its NDC.

Option A2 {*discounting*}

(b)   The host Party to make a corresponding adjustment under the guidance for cooperative approaches referred to in Article 6, paragraph 2 for the full amount of A6.4ERs to be first transferred and the host Party to discount by X per cent at the point of first transfer. The using Party to discount by X per cent the total quantity of A6.4ERs acquired prior to use towards achievement of its NDC. The discounted ITMOs not to be used by any Party towards achievement of its NDC.

Option B {*any or all of a set of methodological approaches from the potential list below*}

(c)   Determining that emission reductions achieved by Article 6, paragraph 4, activities are additional to any that would otherwise occur;

(d)   Applying conservative baselines to the calculation of emission reductions for Article 6, paragraph 4, activities;

(e)   Applying conservative default emission factors to the calculation of emission reductions achieved by Article 6, paragraph 4, activities;

(f)   Limiting the crediting period for an Article 6, paragraph 4, activity to a period shorter than the operational lifetime of the relevant technology or activity, in accordance with the relevant requirements developed by the Supervisory Body.

Option C {*cancellation of A6.4ERs*}

(g)   Voluntary cancellation of A6.4ERs by Parties and stakeholders, including non-State actors;

Option D {*voluntary actions approach*}

(h)   Any other measures selected by participating Parties voluntarily.

XVI.   Avoiding the use of emission reductions by more than one Party

68.   Avoiding the use of emission reductions from the mechanism towards achievement of its NDC by more than one Party, in accordance with Article 6, paragraph 5, to be ensured in accordance with this section.

Option A {*guidance applicable to all emission reductions transferred internationally*}

69.   The guidance relating to corresponding adjustments in the guidance for cooperative approaches referred to in Article 6, paragraph 2 of the Paris Agreement to apply to all emission reductions under the mechanism, when transferred internationally.

Option B {*guidance applicable to emission reductions from sectors/greenhouse gases covered by the NDC*}

70.   The guidance relating to corresponding adjustments in the guidance for cooperative approaches referred to in Article 6, paragraph 2, to apply to emission reductions under the mechanism, that result from a mitigation activity that is included in the sectors/greenhouse gases covered by the host Party's NDC, when those emission reductions are transferred internationally.

71.   The guidance for cooperative approaches referred to in Article 6, paragraph 2 not to apply to emission reductions under the mechanism, if the mitigation activity is not included in the sectors/greenhouse gases covered by the host Party's NDC {*further development may be needed for implementation, for example reporting on such A6.4ERs*}.

Option C {*forwarding based*}

72.   The guidance relating to corresponding adjustments in the guidance for cooperative approaches referred to in Article 6, paragraph 2 is not applicable to the initial forwarding of certified emission reductions from the mechanism registry.

73.   The guidance relating to corresponding adjustments in the guidance for cooperative approaches set out in Article 6, paragraph 2 to apply to any subsequent international transfer of certified emission reductions between registries/ national accounts in the multilateral registry.

Option D {*national allowances based*}

74.   The guidance relating to corresponding adjustments in the guidance for cooperative approaches referred to in Article 6, paragraph 2, to apply to emission reductions issued under the mechanism. A Party with an absolute emission limitation or reduction target in its NDC may then transfer an equivalent quantity of national allowances {*further development may be required for implementation*}.

XVII. Safeguards

A. Uses for purposes other than towards achievement of nationally determined contributions

75.   An A6.4ER to not be used towards achievement of an NDC where it has been or is intended to be used {*potential list below*}:

(a)   Towards international mitigation action outside the UNFCCC;

(b)   Towards voluntary climate actions that are not mandatory in the relevant jurisdiction;

(c)   As a means of demonstrating climate finance provided pursuant to Article 9.

76.   A6.4ERs used for purposes other than towards achievement of NDCs to be subject to a corresponding adjustment in accordance with

Option A {*all accounted for*}

(a)   the guidance for cooperative approaches referred to in Article 6, paragraph 2.

Option B {*only where from within NDC*}

(b)   the guidance for cooperative approaches referred to in Article 6, paragraph 2, if the A6.4ERs were issued from sectors/greenhouse gases/periods covered by an NDC.

{*further development may be required for implementation, for example reference to double counting*}

SBSTA48.Informal.3

B.   Limits {*potential list below*}

Option A {*limits*} {*potential list below*}

77.   The Supervisory Body to issue A6.4ERs in a manner that avoids fluctuations in the prices and quantities available on the international market for A6.4ERs {*further development may be required for implementation*}.

78.   A Party not to transfer/acquire/use A6.4ERs issued for emission reductions achieved in sectors where there is a high degree of uncertainty in emission estimates {*further development may be required for implementation*}.

79.   After the initial transfer from the host Party to the acquiring Party, the acquiring Party not to further transfer A6.4ERs to the host Party or to another Party.

80.   A Party to ensure that speculative transfers of A6.4ERs are avoided {*further development may be required for implementation*}.

81.   A Party not to transfer any quantity of A6.4ERs greater than X {*further development may be required for implementation*}.

82.   A Party not to transfer A6.4ERs in the following ways: {*further development may be required for implementation*}.

83.   A Party's use of A6.4ERs towards achievement of its NDC to be supplemental to domestic action, and domestic action to constitute a significant element of the effort made by each Party towards achievement of its NDC.

84.   A Party not to use towards achievement of its NDC any A6.4ERs issued for emission reductions that were achieved in the period X {*further development may be needed for implementation, including specifying the years*}.

85.   A Party not to use pre-2020 units towards achievement of its NDC {*further development may be required for implementation*}.

86.   A Party not to carry over A6.4ERs exceeding X {*further development may be required for implementation*}.

Option B {*no limits*}

{*no text is required*}

XVIII.   Transition from the Kyoto Protocol to Article 6, paragraph 4

A.   Mitigation activities under the Kyoto Protocol

Option A {*existing CDM/JI activities may become Article 6.4 activities without further conditions*}

87.   The following may be registered as Article 6, paragraph 4 activities {*potential list below*}:

(a)   Projects and programmes of activities registered under joint implementation under Article 6 of the Kyoto Protocol;

(b)   Project activities and programmes of activities registered under the clean development mechanism under Article 12 of the Kyoto Protocol.

Option B {*existing CDM/JI activities may become Article 6.4 activities if they meet certain conditions*}

88.   The following may be registered as Article 6, paragraph 4 activities subject to paragraph 89 {*potential list below*}:

(a)   Projects and programmes of activities registered under joint implementation under Article 6 of the Kyoto Protocol;

(b)   Project activities and programmes of activities registered under the clean development mechanism under Article 12 of the Kyoto Protocol;

89.   To be registered as an Article 6, paragraph 4 activity, the above projects/project activities/programmes of activities to meet the conditions adopted by the Supervisory Body and/or the CMA and/or the following conditions {*potential list below*} {*further development may be required for implementation*}:

(a)   The relevant host Party authorizes such registration.

Option C {*no existing CDM and JI activities may become Article 6.4 activities*}

90.   No activities registered under joint implementation under Article 6 of the Kyoto Protocol or under the clean development mechanism under Article 12 of the Kyoto Protocol may be registered as Article 6, paragraph 4, activities.

B.   Transition of joint implementation emission reduction units

91.   In relation to ERUs,

Option A {*use of ERUs towards achievement of NDCs*}

(a)   ERUs may be used by a Party towards achievement of its NDC.

Option B {*use of ERUs for emission reductions achieved prior to 2020/2021*}

(b)   ERUs issued in relation to emission reductions achieved prior to 1 January 2020/2021 may be used by a Party towards achievement of its NDC.

Option C {*no use of ERUs towards achievement of NDCs*}

(c)   ERUs may not be used by a Party towards achievement of its NDC.

Option D {*issuance of A6.4ERs for JI activities*}

(d)   A6.4ERs may be issued for activities registered under joint implementation under Article 6 of the Kyoto Protocol {*further development may be required for implementation, including in relation to CMP decisions*}.

C.   Transition of clean development mechanism certified emission reductions

92.   In relation to CERs,

Option A {*use of CERs towards achievement of NDCs*}

(a)   CERs may be used by a Party towards achievement of its NDC.

Option B {*use of CERs for emission reductions achieved prior to 2020/2021*}

(b)   CERs issued in relation to emission reductions achieved prior to 1 January 2020/2021 may be used by a Party towards achievement of its NDC.

Option C {*no use of CERs towards achievement of NDCs*}

(c)   CERs may not be used by a Party towards achievement of its NDC.

Option D {*issuance of A6.4ERs for CDM activities*}

(d)   A6.4ERs may be issued for activities registered under the clean development mechanism under Article 12 of the Kyoto Protocol {*further development may be required for implementation, including in relation to CMP decisions*}.

D.   Transition of methodologies

93.   In relation to methodologies under joint implementation under Article 6 of the Kyoto Protocol,

Option A {*use of JI methodologies by Article 6, paragraph 4, activities*}

(a)   baseline and monitoring methodologies etc. under Article 6 of the Kyoto Protocol to be valid for Article 6, paragraph 4, activities {*further development may be required for implementation*}.

Option B {*no use of methodologies by Article 6, paragraph 4, activities*}

{*no text required*}

94.   In relation to methodologies under the clean development mechanism,

Option A {*use of CDM methodologies by Article 6, paragraph 4, activities*}

(a)   baseline and monitoring methodologies etc. under the clean development mechanism under Article 12 of the Kyoto Protocol to be valid for Article 6, paragraph 4, activities {*further development may be required for implementation*}.

Option B {*no use of methodologies by Article 6, paragraph 4, activities*}

{*no text required*}

E.   **Transition of accreditation standards**

Option A {*transition of the accreditation system*}

95.   In relation to accreditation, the standards and procedures etc. for accreditation from the following Kyoto Protocol mechanisms to serve as the basis for the standards and procedures for the mechanism through the adoption of those standard and procedures etc. by the Supervisory Body {*potential list below*}:

(a)   Joint implementation under Article 6 of the Kyoto Protocol;

(b)   The clean development mechanism under Article 12 of the Kyoto Protocol.

Option B {*no transition of the accreditation system*}

{*no text required*}

XIX.   **Adaptation ambition** {*further development may be required for implementation*}

96.   Mitigation co-benefits of adaptation action, including economic diversification.

XX.   **Addressing negative social and economic impacts under Article 4, paragraph 15** {*further development may be required for implementation*}

———————

Framework Convention on
Climate Change

SBSTA48.Informal.4

Subsidiary Body for Scientific and Technological Advice
Forty-eighth session
Bonn, 30 April to 10 May 2018

16 March 2018

Informal document containing the draft elements of the draft decision on the work programme under the framework for non-market approaches referred to in Article 6, paragraph 8, of the Paris Agreement

Informal document by the Chair

Contents

Introduction

A. Mandate

1.   Article 6, paragraph 8, of the Paris Agreement recognizes the importance of integrated, holistic and balanced non-market approaches being available to Parties to assist in the implementation of their nationally determined contributions (NDCs). Article 6, paragraph 9, defines a framework for non-market approaches. By decision 1/CP.21, paragraphs 39 and 40, the Conference of the Parties requested the Subsidiary Body for Scientific and Technological Advice (SBSTA) to undertake a work programme under the framework for non-market approaches and to recommend a draft decision on that work programme for consideration and adoption by the Conference of the Parties serving as the meeting of the Parties to the Paris Agreement at its first session.

2.   At SBSTA 47, to facilitate the deliberations at SBSTA 48, the SBSTA requested the SBSTA Chair to prepare an informal document containing the draft elements of the draft decision on the work programme based on prior submissions by Parties under this agenda sub-item and the third iteration of the informal note prepared by the co-chairs of the relevant agenda item[1] (hereinafter referred to as the third iteration note).

B. Scope

3.   The annex to this informal document contains the draft elements of the draft decision on the work programme prepared by the SBSTA Chair on the basis of the above mandate (hereinafter referred to as the draft elements of the draft decision).

C. Approach

4.   The SBSTA Chair has developed the draft elements of the draft decision based on the third iteration note and previous submissions from the Parties under this agenda sub-item.

5.   The draft elements of the draft decision have, in relation to the third iteration note, sought to:

(a)   Streamline the structure, including removing duplication, without removing elements;

(b)   Bring the elements of each issue together to facilitate discussions at SBSTA 48;

(c)   Develop the language for the implementation of elements from the third iteration note, without developing full text;

(d)   Clarify options and the potential further elements to be considered.

6.   In the draft elements of the draft decision, all paragraphs and sub-paragraphs have been numbered sequentially to make it easier for Parties to identify substantive content of the options when using the informal document to facilitate discussions at SBSTA 48.

7.   Generally, throughout the draft elements of the draft decision, curly brackets containing italicized text ("{*curly brackets containing italicized text*}") are used to provide information about the relevant element.

8.   Where the draft elements of the draft decision contain options, these are labelled as "**Option A**", "**Option B**", etc. To assist navigation of the text, options are followed by a brief indicative narrative, in curly brackets and in bold, italicized text ("{***narrative of the option***}").

9.   Where an element/option has several potential sub-elements, the note "{*potential list below*}" is included just before the list begins, in order to show Parties that they need to consider each sub-element independently, and not as a group of sub-elements. The note "{*further potential list below*}"

---

[1] http://unfccc.int/cooperation_support/cooperative_implementation/items/9644.php and http://unfccc.int/documentation/documents/advanced_search/items/6911.php?priref=600009936.

is used in a similar manner for sub-sub-elements. That note is not used where the sub-elements are a suite and are needed together.

10.   Where it appears that further development of a potential element/option would be required for implementation, the following note is made: "{*further development may be required for implementation*}", and in some cases, further possible action or examples are identified in order to help Parties identify what further development might include.

11.   Where, within a sentence, there are alternatives or choices that may be selected, a forward slash ("/") has been used to indicate those alternatives in the sentence, so that the sentence remains readable as a whole. However, where there is "and/or", this means "and" as well as "or".

12.   Where there is provision for a certain number of events to be organised, members to be appointed, etc. the draft elements of the draft decision use "*X*", "*Y*", "*Z*" etc. to indicate choices that would need to be taken.

13.   The selection of certain options may have implications for other options in other sections of the draft elements of the draft decision. In order to keep the document manageable, not all consequential implications for other parts of the draft elements of the draft decision are indicated. In certain cases, some options are incompatible with some other options in other sections and, where this is particularly acute, the draft elements of the draft decision identify that in curly brackets.

14.   Furthermore, the draft elements of the draft decision cannot assess all the possible ways in which options found in different parts of the text might be combined.

15.   The draft elements of the draft decision also use the phrase "**the A6.8 governance**" as a device for governance of the framework for non-market approaches, and solely for the purposes of keeping the draft elements of the draft decision short and readable (and without prejudice to later definition at a later stage by the SBSTA).

D.   Possible actions by the Subsidiary Body for Scientific and Technological Advice

16.   The SBSTA may wish to consider this informal document, and refine and elaborate the draft elements of the draft decision contained herein.

Annex

Draft elements of the draft decision on the work programme

I.   Preamble

Option A {*list of preambular paragraphs*}{*potential list below*}

Pp1   Recognizing the need to ensure that non-market approaches under the framework for non-market approaches defined in Article 6, paragraph 8, of the Paris Agreement, hereinafter referred to as non-market approaches (NMAs), to aim to promote mitigation and adaptation ambition,

Pp2   Also recognizing the need to ensure that NMAs provide incentives for progression beyond participating Parties' then current nationally determined contributions,

Pp3   Further recognizing the need to ensure that NMAs support participating Parties in meeting their mitigation objectives,

Option B {*no list of preambular paragraphs*}

{*no text required*}

II.   Principles

Option A {*list of principles*}

1.   The following principles to guide the implementation of the framework for non-market approaches referred to in Article 6, paragraph 9, of the Paris Agreement[1] (hereinafter referred to as the framework) and the work programme under the framework for non-market approaches referred to in decision 1/CP.21, paragraph 39 (hereinafter referred to as the work programme) {*potential list below*}:

(a)   Principles for the framework {*further potential list below*}:

    (i)   Provide opportunities for sharing experience and best practices;

    (ii)   Preserve national prerogatives in relation to sustainable development in the implementation of NMAs;

    (iii)   Provide enhanced support to developing countries through finance and capacity-building for the implementation of NMAs;

    (iv)   Operate within the context of Article 6 as a whole;

(b)   Principles for NMAs that are under the framework {*further potential list below*}:

    (i)   NMAs to contribute to the objectives of the Paris Agreement referred to in its Article 2;

    (ii)   In accordance with Article 6, paragraph 1, Parties may participate in NMAs on a voluntary basis;

    (iii)   In accordance with Article 6, paragraph 1, NMAs allow for higher ambition of participating Parties in their mitigation and adaptation actions;

    (iv)   Pursuant to Article 6, paragraph 1, NMAs should promote environmental integrity;

    (v)   In accordance with Article 6, paragraph 8, NMAs are integrated, holistic and balanced and are to assist in the implementation of nationally determined contributions (NDCs);

---

[1] References to "Article" are to articles of the Paris Agreement, unless otherwise specified.

4

(vi)   In accordance with Article 6, paragraph 8, NMAs promote sustainable development and poverty eradication;

(vii)   In accordance with Article 6, paragraph 8(a), NMAs to aim to promote mitigation and adaptation ambition;

(viii) In accordance with Article 6, paragraph 8(b), NMAs to aim to enhance public and private sector participation in the implementation of NDCs;

(ix)   In accordance with Article 6, paragraph 8(c), NMAs to aim to enable opportunities for coordination across instruments and relevant institutional arrangements;

(x)   In accordance with the preamble to the Paris Agreement, NMAs should not infringe human rights and other rights;

(xi)   NMAs should provide incentives for progression beyond participating Parties' then current NDCs pursuant to Article 4, paragraph 3;

(xii)   NMAs should maintain harmony among environmental, social and economic dimensions of sustainable development, taking into consideration Article 4, paragraphs 7 and 15;

(xiii) NMAs should assist participating Parties in implementing the objectives of their NDCs;

(xiv)   Parties participating in NMAs to ensure that the NMAs do not duplicate work under the Convention, the Kyoto Protocol, the Paris Agreement or other multilateral forums;

(xv)   NMAs are not reliant on market-based approaches but may provide incentives for domestic mitigation actions in the form of payments without transfer of units;

(xvi)   NMAs should ensure manageable sustainable development transition for all Parties;

(xvii) NMAs should avoid unilateral measures and employ non-discriminatory practices.

Option B {*list of preambular principles*}

{*see Option A of section I above*}

Option C {*no principles*}

{*no text required*}

III.   Definitions

2.   For the purpose of this decision on the work programme under the framework for non-market approaches referred to in decision 1/CP.21, paragraph 40 (hereinafter referred to as this decision), the definitions contained in Article 1 and the provisions referred to in Article 17 to apply. Furthermore, {*potential list below*}:

(a)   An "**internationally transferred mitigation outcome**" and "**ITMO**" have the meaning given to it in the guidance on cooperative approaches referred to in Article 6, paragraph 2;

(b)   A "**nationally determined contribution limitation quotient unit**" has the meaning given to it in the rules, modalities and procedures for the mechanism established by Article 6, paragraph 4.

{*further definitions may be required for implementation*}

IV.   Objectives/purposes

A.   Framework

3.   The objectives/purposes of the framework are {*potential list below*}:

(a)   To contribute to the objectives of the Paris Agreement as set out in its Article 2;

(b)   To allow for higher ambition of Parties in their mitigation and adaptation actions and to promote sustainable development and environmental integrity as referred to in Article 6, paragraph 1;

(c)   To promote NMAs as referred to in Article 6, paragraph 9.

B.   Work programme

4.   The objectives/purposes of the work programme are to consider how to enhance linkages and create synergy between, inter alia, mitigation, adaptation, finance, technology transfer and capacity-building and how to facilitate the implementation and coordination of NMAs as referred to in decision 1/CP.21, paragraph 39.

V.   Scope of the framework

A.   Non-market approaches under the framework

1.   Aims of non-market approaches as referred to in Article 6, paragraph 8(a), (b) and (c)

5.   Each NMA to:

Option A {*meet all the aims*}

(a)   aim to achieve all of the aims of NMAs referred to in Article 6, paragraph 8(a), (b) and (c).

Option B { *meet at least one of the aims*}

(b)   aim to achieve at least one of the aims of NMAs referred to in Article 6, paragraph 8 (a), (b) and (c).

Option C {*apply in the context of Article 6, paragraphs 2 and 4*}

(c)   apply in the context of Article 6, paragraph 2, and Article 6, paragraphs 4–7.

Option D {*no reference to the aims*}

{*no text required*}

2.   Voluntary cooperation between Parties in the implementation of their NDCs

6.   Each NMA to {*potential list below*}:

(a)   Involve more than one participating Party in voluntary cooperation that is bilateral, regional or multilateral;

(b)   Involve more than one participating Party and public and private sector participant(s);

(c)   Encourage voluntary cooperation between Parties;

(d)   Aim to assist in the implementation of NDCs of the participating Parties.

3.   Relationship with internationally transferred mitigation outcomes referred to in Article 6, paragraph 2

7.   Each NMA not to {*potential list below*}:

(a)   Create or issue any ITMOs/nationally determined contribution limitation quotient units;

(b)   Transfer any ITMOs;

(c)   Involve any market-based approaches.

4. **Integrated, holistic and balanced nature of NMAs**

8. Each NMA to {*potential list below*}:

(a) Cover more than one of each of the following areas: mitigation, adaptation, finance, technology transfer and capacity-building;

(b) Avoid duplication with the work of subsidiary and constituted bodies under or related to the Convention, the Kyoto Protocol and the Paris Agreement and other multilateral forums;

(c) Aim to promote sustainable development and poverty eradication in accordance with Article 6, paragraph 8.

VI. Governance of the framework

Option A {*SBSTA agenda item*}

9. The Subsidiary Body for Scientific and Technological Advice (SBSTA) to implement the framework and the work programme at its first/second/first and second sessional period meeting each year, with its first meeting taking place at its X session.

Option B {*task force*}

10. A task force for the framework (hereinafter referred to as the task force) is hereby established to implement the framework and the work programme.

11. The Chair of the SBSTA to convene the task force, which will meet twice a year in conjunction with the sessions of the SBSTA {*further development may be required for implementation, including when the task force will meet for the first time*}.

12. The task force to comprise X members as follows:

(a) X members from Parties to the Paris Agreement, with balanced regional representation, appointed by the President of the Conference of the Parties (COP)/elected by the Conference of the Parties serving as the meeting of the Parties to the Paris Agreement (CMA);

(b) X members from social organizations nominated by Parties, with balanced regional representation;

(c) X members from the Board of the Green Climate Fund (GCF), the Technology Executive Committee (TEC) and the Paris Committee on Capacity-building {*further development may be required for implementation, including consideration of members from the other operating entities of the financial mechanism*}.

13. Two co-chairs of the task force to be appointed, one being a member from a developing country Party and one from a developed country Party.

{*further development may be required for implementation, including functions of the task force, rules of procedure, budget and workplan, and membership issues such as nomination, qualifications and term of office, quorum and participation of observers*}

Option C {*permanent forum held in conjunction with the meetings of the subsidiary bodies*}

14. A forum for the framework (hereinafter referred to as the forum) is hereby established to implement the framework and the work programme.

15. The Chair of the SBSTA to convene the forum, which will meet in conjunction with the first/second/first and second sessional period meeting of the SBSTA.

{*further development may be required for implementation, including when the forum will meet for the first time*}

Option D {*existing committees and structures (e.g. Adaptation Fund, Standing Committee on Finance) with or without expansion of their terms of reference*}

16. The existing constituted bodies under the Convention, the Kyoto Protocol and the Paris Agreement that carry out activities relevant to the work programme activities under the framework to:

(a)   Implement the relevant work programme activities under the framework, to the extent possible within their existing terms of reference and the availability of their financial resources; and/or

(b)   Review their terms of reference and work programme activities, where necessary, with a view to enabling them to carry out the relevant work programme activities under the framework in the context of the implementation of the framework and the work programme and, where appropriate, recommend draft revisions to their terms of reference and work programme for consideration and adoption by the COP, the CMA, or the Conference of the Parties serving as the meeting of the Parties to the Kyoto Protocol (CMP), as appropriate, at its *X*, *Y* and *Z* session, respectively.

{further development may be required for implementation, including processes whereby the COP, the CMP or the CMA request the relevant existing bodies to implement the related work programme activities under the framework and/or to review their terms of references based on recommendations from the SBSTA}

Option E {*Committee for the Future*}

17.   The Committee for the Future is hereby established. The Committee for the Future to implement/supervise the framework and the work programme, under the authority and guidance of the CMA.

{further development may be required for implementation, including functions of the Committee for the Future, rules of procedure, budget and workplan, and composition of the Committee for the Future including membership, nomination, qualifications and term of office, and on chairs, quorum and participation of observers. In addition, on how often the Committee for the Future will meet and when it will meet for the first time}

Option F {*Party determines its own governance structures*}

18.   Any Party may establish its own governance arrangements for the framework in order to implement the framework and supervise its national work programme under the framework within the Party.

19.   In order to facilitate the implementation, each participating Party is encouraged to voluntarily develop its national work programme, determine NMAs within the Party and report on the implementation of the NMAs in accordance with paragraph 30 below *{see option B of section IX (Reporting)}*.

{further development may be required for implementation, including in relation to other sections of this draft decision}

Option G {*through the work programme, jointly by the SBSTA and the SBI, in consultation and with existing UNFCCC bodies*}

20.   The Subsidiary Body for Implementation (SBI) and the SBSTA to jointly coordinate the framework and the work programme, including through the technical examination process on mitigation referred to in decision 1/CP.21, paragraph 109 and that on adaptation referred to in decision 1/CP.21, paragraph 124.

{further development may be required for implementation, including any decisions to enable the technical examination process post-2020. In addition, on how, when and how often the SBI and the SBSTA will jointly meet}

21.   The secretariat to, in consultation with the Technology Executive Committee (TEC) and the Climate Technology Centre and Network and in accordance with their respective mandates, conduct the technical examination process on mitigation.

{further development may be required for implementation, including reporting from the secretariat to the SBI and the SBSTA}

22.   The Adaptation Committee to, in consultation with the Standing Committee on Finance, the TEC, the Least Developed Countries Expert Group (LEG) and observer constituencies and with support from the secretariat, conduct the technical examination process on adaptation.

SBSTA48.Informal.4

{further development may be required for implementation, including how the terms of reference of the Adaptation Committee would be revised if they do not cover relevant work programme activities under the framework and reporting from the Adaptation Committee to the SBI and the SBSTA}

Option H {*no organizational arrangements for the framework*}

{no text required}

VII. Modalities of the work programme

Option A {*collective approach*}

23.   The governance of the framework referred to in section VI above (Governance of the framework) (hereinafter referred to as the A6.8 governance) to, in implementing the work programme activities referred to in section VIII (Work programme activities), apply the following modalities of the work programme, as appropriate*{potential list below}*:

(a)   Workshops;

(b)   Regular meetings with public and private sector participants, including technical experts, business, civil society organizations and financial institutions, and the subsequent publication of the outcomes of the regular meetings;

(c)   A web-based repository of submissions from Parties, observer organizations and public and private sector participants;

(d)   A public web-based platform that facilitates identification of opportunities to enhance linkages and create synergies between, inter alia, mitigation, adaptation, finance, technology transfer and capacity-building;

(e)   A public web-based platform that aims to match the needs of participating Parties and public and private sector participants for the development and implementation of NMAs with the support offered by other Parties and other public and private sector participants;

(f)   A public web-based registry for the Adaptation Benefit Mechanism;

(g)   A public web-based registry for the environmental balance index;

(h)   Technical papers and synthesis reports prepared by the secretariat;

(i)   Coordination, where needed, between the A6.8 governance and the forum on the impact of the implementation of response measures referred to in decision 1/CP.21, paragraph 33 *{further development may be required for implementation}*.

Option B {*national approach*}{*potential list below*}

24.   Parties voluntarily developing and implementing national work programmes in accordance with paragraphs 18 and 19 above and public and private sector participants developing and implementing NMAs within the Parties may make submissions on their work programmes to the SBSTA, as appropriate *{see Option F of section VI (Governance of the framework)}*.

Option C {*negative list of the modalities of the work programme*}

25.   The A6.8 governance to, in implementing the work programme activities referred to in section VIII (Work programme activities), refrain from applying the following modalities of the work programme*{further development may be required for implementation}*:.

Option D {*decide modalities after decision on the work programme*}

26.   The SBSTA to develop and recommend draft modalities of the work programme for consideration and adoption by the CMA at its second session (November 2019), taking into account recommendations from the A6.8 governance.

SBSTA48.Informal.4

VIII. Work programme activities

A. Stepped activities

27.   The A6.8 governance to implement the following stepped activities in the period $X–Y$ with a view to achieving the objectives/purposes of the work programme referred to in section IV. B (Work programme) {*potential list below*}:

(a)   STEP 1: Identify areas of focus by:

Option A {*outputs of the technical examination process*}

(i)   drawing on the outputs of the technical examination processes on mitigation and adaptation.

Option B {*guidance for the areas of focus*}

(ii)   developing guidance for the areas of focus.

Option C {*guidance for the areas of focus plus identifying the specific areas in this decision*}

(iii)   developing guidance for the areas of focus, including {*further potential list below*}:

    a.   Joint mitigation and adaptation for the integral and sustainable management of forests;

    b.   Social ecological resilience;

    c.   Avoidance of greenhouse gas emissions;

    d.   Ecosystem-based adaptation;

    e.   Integrated water management;

    f.   Energy efficiency schemes;

(b)   STEP 2: Identify existing activities in the areas of focus that are considered to be NMAs in accordance with section V.A above(Non-market approaches under the framework);

(c)   STEP 3: Identify existing linkages, synergies, coordination and implementation in relation to those NMAs, and identify, record and evaluate the positive and other experience from those NMAs {*further development may be required for implementation*};

(d)   STEP 4: Identify opportunities to enhance the existing linkages, create synergies, and facilitate coordination and implementation of NMAs, including in the local, national and global context {*further development may be required for implementation*};

(e)   STEP 5: Assess the results of the previous steps and develop and recommend conclusions on how to enhance existing linkages and create synergies for consideration by the CMA at its X session {*further development may be required for implementation, including whether to recommend conclusions on how to facilitate the implementation and coordination of NMAs*};

(f)   STEP 6: Take action to enhance linkages and create synergies while avoiding duplication of its activities with those under the subsidiary and constituted bodies under or related to the Convention, the Kyoto Protocol and the Paris Agreement and other multilateral forums {*further development may be required for implementation, including whether to take action to facilitate the implementation and coordination of NMAs*}.

B. Cross-step activities

28.   In implementing the stepped activities referred to in section VIII.A (Stepped activities), the A6.8 governance to, where appropriate, also implement the following cross-step activities that contribute to implementing one or more other step(s) referred to above{*potential list below*}:

(a)   Identifying, developing and implementing tools, including {*further potential list below*}:

(i)   A public web-based platform that aims to match the needs of participating Parties and public and private sector participants for the development and implementation of

NMAs, including finance, technology transfer and capacity-building, with the support offered by other Parties and other public and private sector participants;

(ii) A UNFCCC web-based platform to register, officially recognize and exchange information on NMAs;

(iii) A web-based clearing house mechanism to enable participating Parties and public and private sector participants to identify opportunities for collaboration in developing and implementing NMAs;

(iv) A public list of activities that should not form a part of the work programme activities;

(v) Tools to address possible negative social and economic impacts of activities under Article 6;

(vi) Tools to measure and monitor the implementation of NMAs in the context of sustainable development and poverty eradication;

(b) Identifying and sharing relevant information, best practices, lessons learned and case studies for the development and implementation of NMAs, including on {*further potential list below*}:

(i) Opportunities for replication of successful NMAs;

(ii) Enabling environments and policy frameworks for the development and implementation of NMAs;

(iii) Successful cross-cutting policy and regulatory approaches to developing and implementing NMAs;

(iv) Barriers to and incentives for:

a. Enhancing the engagement of and addressing the needs of the private sector, exposed and impacted sectors and communities in NMAs;

b. Achieving a just transition of the workforce;

(v) Measures related to education, training, public awareness, public participation and public access to information to promote greater mitigation and adaptation ambition;

(vi) Approaches to leveraging and generating mitigation and adaptation co-benefits;

(c) Developing and implementing the Adaptation Benefit Mechanism;

(d) Developing and implementing the work programme of the Committee for the Future, including arrangements for the environmental balance index.

IX. Reporting

Option A {*reporting by the A6.8 governance to the CMA*}

29. The A6.8 governance to report to each session of the CMA on the progress and outcomes of the work programme, including {*potential list below*}:

(a) A summary of the best practices for developing and implementing NMAs;

(b) A summary of the support available to Parties for developing and implementing NMAs;

(c) Recommendations to the GCF and other financial institutions on how to enhance support to NMAs.

Option B {*reporting by Parties on the implementation of NMAs under Article 13*}

30. A Party involved in implementing NMAs, to report on the implementation in accordance with Article 13, including, as relevant {*potential list below*}:

(a) How the NMAs promoted mitigation and adaptation ambition in its NDC, enhanced public and private sector participation in the implementation and enabled opportunities for coordination across instruments and relevant institutional arrangements;

(b)   Confirmation that implementation of the NMAs did not involve any transfer of ITMOs;

(c)   How the NMAs contributed to sustainable development and poverty eradication;

(d)   Information on support provided, received and needed on finance, technology transfer and capacity-building for implementing the NMAs.

Option C {*both Option A and B*}

{*see Options A and B above*}

Option D {*decide reporting after decision on the work programme*}

31.   The SBSTA to develop and recommend draft modalities for the reporting under the framework for consideration and adoption by CMA at its second session (November 2019) taking into account recommendations from the A6.8 governance.

Option E {*use other relevant reporting modalities under the Paris Agreement*}

{*further development may be required for implementation*}

Option F {*no reporting under the framework*}

{*no text*}

X. Review

A. Review of annual report

32.   The CMA to review the report from the A6.8 governance referred to in section IX (Reporting) on an annual basis and provide guidance, where appropriate {*applies for Options A and C in section IX (Reporting)*}.

B. Review of the work programme

33.   The CMA to review this decision, including the work programme's objectives/purposes and governance/modalities/activities:

Option A {*provide recommendations to Parties after the periodic review*}

(a)   and provide guidance to the A6.8 governance every X years, beginning at its sixth session (November 2023), taking into account recommendations from the A6.8 governance and the outcomes of the global stocktake.

Option B {*review in 2023 in order to improve effectiveness with a view to adopting a decision on the outcome of the review*}

(b)   by no later than its sixth session (November 2023) with a view to adopting a decision on the outcome of the review by no later than at that session {*further development may be required for implementation*}.

12

www.ingramcontent.com/pod-product-compliance
Lightning Source LLC
Chambersburg PA
CBHW041120280326
41928CB00061B/3468